Her Heart Song

Poetry and Short Stories of a Healing Heart

Izzy Lala

Her Heart Song.

Izzy Lala
2020

Contents

Dedication

Dedicated to my mother, Delilah Ward, whose light and love have always lifted me up from darkness

Preface

What is a heart song? I am convinced it is a song or poem that is the expression of a person's inner essence. The expression of a person's underlying purpose. Be it fiction or not, I have decided to compile a collection of poetry accompanied by underlying stories that exemplify this expression.

Her Heart Song is a collection of excerpted fiction stories with interlaced poetry. Weaving in and out of time and space, it tells a girl's story behind each of her most compelling poems. This book has seven sections; each beginning with the poem that most embodies the chapter. It follows the timeline of a girl's life and includes flashbacks of brief, magnified moments as well as poetry added to expand the storyline. Behind the story at hand are people and events that are the inspiration for the character's poems. In essence, each of these stories has impacted her enough to pick up a pen and write her heart song in poems. This book is an unfinished tale that gives a window into the longer story soon to come.

Her Heart Song

I 'm standing on stage in an auditorium packed with people who have come just to hear me speak. At least that is what it feels like at Poet's Café – a mecca for poets in Downtown Sacramento. They have asked me to be the featured artist for the evening. So here I am, poised, with a colorful scarf wrapped around my head like I have just conjured up my most urban roots and now they are manifested in front of a crowd, listening intently for what story will sprout from them.

"I've written poetry since the age of seven," I tell the audience. "I still remember sitting on my bunk bed, spilling my most inner thoughts on a small, gold-trimmed journal with a lock and key. I still remember my mom reading my poems from elementary school with a smile on her face and saying how good it was – that I was her gifted child. But, as life may have it, sometimes gifts are buried or locked away like that journal with secret writings."

The audience looks at me with wondering eyes, waiting for what will come next from the new artist on the platform.

"Poetry is like a window into the heart," I say. "It can tell a story, if but in a short, few eloquent words. So here, I have managed to compile the stories that have led me to the very poetry written from my heart…"

I
Poverty

Poverty

We had no money
But the house was always full
With kids running through those halls of thin walls
You could hear the laughing on the other side
And the growling stomach would subside
We had no money
And welfare was funny
Because, we all waited for the first to come –
After splurging throughout the month
On food that never lasted till the end
We always knew when the month would begin again
Because tacos were on the table and my mom's mind a little more stable,
And we laughed a little harder.
My mom always said: "we may not have much, but at least we have love"
And embarrassed as I was
Of a home with no furniture
And a fridge with no food
I still laughed with my brother and sister
And ran with them through the dark halls of borderline poverty
And giggled in the face of emptiness and disgrace –
For we had more than that empty fridge
My mom said it to begin with,
That an empty heart is worse than an empty stomach,
For at least an empty stomach can fill up with a few tacos
But what of an empty heart?
No - family to fill that empty house
No - parents to feed those empty mouths
No - laughter on the other side
We had no money
But our hearts were always full

And food was secondary to our soul –
For laughter feeds the soul
Can't you hear that laughter call
For poverty is a choice in us all

Of all my mom's children, I look the most like her. My curly brown hair frames an oval face of almond brown eyes the shape of my mother's, her long distinctive nose and thin lips made for smiling. I'm the youngest of three girls and the older sister of a brother just one year younger than me. Where we grew up, in a small underprivileged neighborhood in Sacramento - the city of trees - the seasons always changed. The first season - which we deem spring – the flowers always blossomed; some red, some pink, some white, all beautiful and unique in their ways. The summer is when they needed water the most as the scorching Sacramento sun often wilted them if not showered enough. My mom would often go out to water them in her dingy, torn jeans to make sure they stayed alive as long as possible. She kept them alive until they went dormant in the winter months as the cold winds picked up. It never snowed in Sacramento, but it was often cold enough to bundle in our puff coats as our noses turned red and our cheeks flushed in our heatless home, and the flowers no longer blossomed in front of our house. Instead, winter left only their bare thorn branches as fallen petals now disintegrated into the earth. They were long winters as we waited for spring to come around, when my mom would take care of her flowers again, watering them and nurturing them enough to bring them back to life.

When the first petal fell, I knew winter was coming soon.

Year 1990

M y brother and sister are sleeping in a sleeping bag on the floor next to my mom and me in the cool of a fall evening. She is reading me a children's story. Her voice is soft as a feather on skin and words gently sail from her lips and into my young ears as she reads the bold words on glossy pages. I cradle in my mom's arms as she sits upright on the wall where shadows surround us, generated by a dim lamplight on the floor.

We are homeless.

My mom said we had to move here because the landlord was selling our house. But my oldest sister - who is old enough to live with her boyfriend - said we are homeless. At first, I didn't believe her. I believed my mom who also had plans for us staying in a hotel before we moved to my aunt's. My sister said it is a shelter, not a hotel.

"A homeless shelter is not a fucking hotel," she said as we drove in her Mitsubishi Cruiser to her house for a couple days while my mom was figuring out what to do about our displaced case.

My sisters were sitting in the front and my brother and me in the back while my oldest sister went on and on about my mom using all our money on smoking up drugs.

I wanted to cry thinking about my mom who was at the house alone gathering the rest of our belongings. A silent tear escaped, and my sister looked at me from the rearview mirror with sorrowful eyes.

"Eliza, I'm sorry," she says. "I didn't mean to make you cry, but mom is making bad choices."

I covered my eyes because more tears were streaming down like an uncontrollable volcano. I wanted to run far away. I wanted to hide in my mom's arms again, hear her soothing voice and feel her puffy curls brush across the side of my tear-stained face.

...

Before we moved to my aunt's house on the other side of the tracks, my sister, brother and I played with the neighbors in the white house down the street. Our house was dark-muddy brown and four or five houses down. My mom let us play until after hours when the sun died, and the darkness restored, and the streetlights lit pink and yellow flames. When we returned to our dim home - where my mom rarely flipped the light switch - my mom would be cleaning the kitchen like she had not cleaned in months. Her rapid scrubbing gestures moving from tile to stove to table. The sanitation always occurred the first of the month when paychecks came in and parents disappeared mysteriously.

All the kids in the neighborhood's faces lit up like lottery winners the first of the month. Welfare checks and food stamps meant clothes and food we did not have the rest of the month. A couple of days would go, and my mother's absence would grow, but when she came home, she had brown paper bags of groceries for tacos only at the dawn of the new month. She'd shuffle into the kitchen and light up the gas stove until it sizzled and cracked. Then she'd start dicing tomatoes, onions, and lettuce. Soon the whole house smelled of fried tortillas and taco seasoning. After, we'd eat like kings and queens, but I'd watch my mom sneak away and retreat to the dark backroom where we were forbidden.

Our friends and their mom from down the street would come over, and us kids would play marbles on the clean floor while the moms fled to the cryptic room. I didn't ask questions about my mom. I was too involved with marbles, and I suppose that's just how we are - the children of a mysterious mother who bans us from secret things in a dark room. But when midnight strikes, my eyes were too heavy, and I heard only creeping footsteps in the background before falling into the blackness of deep sleep.

...

My mom is a single mother and has been for all the years I can remember. I see my dad on some occasions, but mostly it is just my mom and us three kids. She used to walk us to and from school spring, summer, fall and winter as we told her tales of elementary school. These days, she nods and partly smiles as if her mind is in another world when she picks my brother and me up from the bus stop down the street from our aunt's. Since moving in with my aunt, she has become even more of a recluse and downcast. Her black puffy curls hang around her face as she looks to the pavement while I tell her about my teacher who has complimented my writing. "I'm so happy, sweetheart," she says, then we walk in silence back to my aunt's house behind the liquor store.

...

In the cool of the fall night, when the sun shines no more and warmth has shifted to drafts of air, I see my mom circling the newspaper with a pencil. Her back is against the wall again, and she is sitting upright with the lamplight by her side that ignites small print on grey paper. I hear the shuffle of the pages turning as I rest my head on a flat pillow by her side. My young ears pierce at the sound of hollering in the other room. It sounds like my aunt and uncle's voice yelling on top of one another. My wide eyes turn towards the dull-beige wall as my heart rate speeds up and pumps through my chest into my ears and I hope my mom does not go out there. They bicker often. I can only imagine it is the hidden things in the darkroom that exacerbate the screams. It has become something of the norm to hear such angry pitches, and I have become accustomed to animosity in a household that is not my mom's.

As long as my mom is with us in the shabby small room, fear somehow subsides.

I shut my eyes and pretend to sleep as I hear the pencil continuing to circle like chalk on a chalkboard. My eyes are beginning to get heavy and are shutting like those windows that keep the cool breeze outside when I hear the door creak.

...

My brother and I are sitting together on the yellow school bus going back to my aunt's house. I see my mom at the bus stop waiting in her worn jeans to pick us up. I feel a buzz like a bee inside when I see her on that fall day where the leaves have fallen to the ground and piled up on the curbs. When I hop off, my mom's warm arms wrap around my cold body. My mom, brother and I walk down the gritty street as my brother kicks up the colorful leaves as we pass by houses with wilted grass, and my mom rests her hand on my back. Her other arm carries my backpack of books she'll read me later that night as has become our ritual.

"I have something to tell you guys," she says as my brother and I stare wide-eyed like we are waiting for a Christmas gift to open.

"What?" My brother asks as his eyes - much bigger than mine - wait for her to unwrap the gift.

"We're moving! I found a place."

"Yes!" My brother exclaims without hesitation.

"When?" I ask as excited as my mom looks.

"Next week. On the first."

I smile giddy and we all walk back to the cramped bedroom my aunt loaned us for a couple of weeks.

...

We roll up in my grandmother's lent old mustang with our belongings of clothes and dishes and blankets stuffed in the trunk. It is all three of us kids staring out the small triangle window in the backseat, wide-eyed and day dreamy. We stare and sit silent and still as my mom turns the corner and my brother's hands are on the side door like he is just about to jump out.

We roll up to a green-colored house - a dull green as broccoli - and shingles missing along the front of the house. I beam, and we all jump out of the car. My brother is nearly running towards the unpainted wood door as my mom follows with a soft smile on her face and turns the key to unlock it.

We rush into the dark hall nearly trampling each other. I follow my sister and brother into the living room where a bright curtain-less window sheds light on an old brick fireplace. We circle around the room and into the tiny kitchen where a black stove exists and a dull white kitchen sink with dark mold in the crevices. I glance back to look at my mom who is still smiling her humble smile.

"Like it?" She asks.

"Yeah!" My brother exclaims.

"Yeah," I say softly, relieved that we are not sleeping on the floor of my aunt's room or in a homeless hotel.

I see my mom stare at me with eyes that reflect light from the living room window. Her face - now tilted down towards me - has become the face of an innocent, smiling girl. And suddenly, it is like my heart has lifted just like her smile.

We go out to the age-old mustang and begin to pull out our belongings.

Later we sit in the living room on the brown, scruffy floor and my mom grabs wood and newspapers and begins to light a fire in our new fireplace.

A green sleeping bag is bundled up in the corner, and my mom grabs it and swings it open like a blanket for a picnic in the park. We all climb on. My sister and brother lay on one side of my mom and me on the other side, and the fire burns pink and yellow flames in the dark.

Cradled Words

On a sheet-less mattress, in a shabby-brown bedroom, my mom read me a story. It was from a children's book – a fantasy one – that lifts the imagination and takes you to some far-off world. I was seven years old and I loved reading. I loved holding the hardcovered books with colorful pages igniting my senses - like fireworks exploding in the eyes of a wide-eyed child.

The pictures were followed by large-printed words that brought them to life. But more than the words on pages, I loved the way my mom read these stories. How she lifted them off the page and into my ears. The way her voice was soothing, soft and slow. It was the only voice of its kind in a house filled with bickering and harsh words - enough to make a child run away and hide.

Away into my mom's arms - that's where I'd hide. We were homeless at the time and my aunt had taken us into her small duplex – all three of us kids and my mom. It was a house of strife with fires ignited with every bitter word spit; unlike words softly floating from my mother's lips like a whispered lullaby.

We lived in one bedroom – my mom, my siblings and I – a room that was safe as long as my mom was there.

I cradled there with my mom under a dim lamplight as shadows surrounded us as a listening audience. My mom flipped pages slowly as I hung onto every last word she read; tuning in attentively, hoping to read like her one day.

When she finished the book, she said, "I love you like the moon loves the stars."

"I love you like the rainbow loves the sun," I returned, not knowing it would be the first poem I had ever spoken.

Maybe it was because the book spawned my imagination; maybe it was because my imagination was wild; or maybe, it was because my mom inspired me to imagine happier places.

She'd smile a warm smile and kiss me on my forehead goodnight.

We practiced this poetic-ritual often while we were in a place that was far from happy: a place my mom had no control. Little did she know her presence and soft-spoken words created a sanctuary for me where my imagination could run wildly away from darkness.

Voices

The small voice inside is my guide
Sounds like every mother's love
Clicking the night light on
For a child's fear of the dark
When all around
Voices holler
The sound of a stumbling father
Throwing empty beer cans
"Crash"
Against a wall
The sound of drunken rage colliding
With reality
Empties his stomach of poison mixed with children
Then goes out again
Voices holler
My name in slurs
From inside that corner bar
From the open door
Tells me of bright sealing lights
Illuminating dancing shadows
Feet moving swift as the boom, boom
Beat
The thudding vibrations of desire
Dancing on the dirty footprint floor
They have been here before
Dancing with warm pleasure running through
Their veins
Before the cold bed of shame
Voices holler
The moaning sound in the night
As strangers whisper every word
That tingles a spine
The smell of liquor on heavy breath
The panting for air – life's source
Running

Away
From
Them
Voices holler
My name in the midnight
Tells me I am chosen
Addiction DNA passed through blood
Of a mother, father, family
If you
Listen to the calling
It shouts from the halfway house
Down the street
Tells me there is a room built there
Just for me
But it is the voice within
That leaves the light on
Always leading me back
To
A place
Of peace

Year 1994

I'm twelve years old and it is Saturday, the first of the month. My mom is manically cleaning the sinks and countertops, and she has just finished mopping the kitchen floor. The kitchen is always sparkling clean the first of the month. But as the month dwindles, my mom lays on a sleeping bag while us three kids watch the black and white TV on the floor next to her because we have no couch to sit on.

My mom is a mystery. Always has been. She goes from highs to lows as the month trails on. I often sense something cold and strange in the air that frightens me, but I can't put my finger on it. I just see the telling of a jobless mother, with depleting energy and a bagful of untold stories. But I forget about it because every other mother in our neighborhood has the same story.

...

The following day, my sister and cousin are on the old wooden bunk bed, and they are whispering when I walk in. No other furniture exists in our room, and the summer sun streams from the window ahead with tacked cloth made curtain.

They both turn my way.

I ask what they are talking about - like a little sister would - and they look at each other with wondering eyes. The whole room shifts to silence and I feel the thing in the air that scares me again. I wait for them to answer as if I am waiting to be accepted into some secret society no one knows about.

"Eliza, mom's on drugs," my sister finally lets out.

"Oh."

I don't know what else to say. Suddenly, I am in the secret society and cannot get out.

"Yeah, that's what they do in the garage. That's why mom acts weird sometimes."

I don't say a word. I just think about my mom and my heart is confused and worried at the same time; but I don't say a word. Suddenly, the floating fiction in the air is pinpointed and has taken form, in fact. My almond-shaped eyes are opened to a new world: a world my mother is in.

...

Tomorrow, my mom said we are going to a home church on the other side of town. It's my dad's friend who has invited us. My dad has come to stay with us for a time. He's a drinker and has been known to abandon his family to drink whiskey with his friends. But he says one of his friends has been saved and turned Christian, and so we going to the other side of town to visit the home church he attends.

I'm excited because I've never been to a church before. I'm thrilled to go anywhere since we rarely do as a family. It's usually just my sister, brother and I playing outside until after dusk with the neighbors and an old, frayed basketball.

Tonight, we're playing with each other, running and dribbling up and down the driveway. My brother shoots the ball into the basket of our makeshift hoop, and I am on our front steps waiting my turn. I look up into the window of our kitchen. I see my mom moving frantically, wiping down counters and cupboards like we are having company over in two minutes and she forgot to deep clean. I think about what my cousin and sister told me. I see dots of addiction and behavior connected and suddenly my mom makes sense.

My mom has no friends besides her siblings who retreat to a garage of spider webs and rats crawling on the wood boards of the roof. They don't seem to care as long as it is behind closed doors.

My brother and I play until after hours when the streetlights come on, bouncing the ball up and down with pounding sounds. It touches concrete then rises high in the steamy night air, and it seems so free out here.

When we are too fatigued to play and our faces have become red and damp with sweat, we go back inside to watch the small, square TV light up the walls and wait for my mom to come to join us. This could be hours.

My brother and I stay up watching one of those old TV series until our lids are too heavy to stay open, and I let out my final breath of air before falling into a deep sleep. Soon, my mom will come in and carry me to my bunk bed, and I'll faintly open my lids as she turns the nightlight on by my side and whispers, "Love you, with all my heart."

...

Sunday morning my mom is up, and she is in the bathroom. I immediately remember church. I hurry to the bathroom where my mom has the door open and is fluffing her black curly hair.

"Are we still going to church?" I ask.

"Yeah, you kids get ready," my mom says, looking down to the spotted tile blankly. Her cheeks are sunken, but she puts a reddish, pink powder on, and they flush as if she has just applied paint to a blank canvas. She looks into the stained mirror still not smiling.

I go put on my dark denim and nice flower top my grandmother bought me from the thrift store she works at. I go to the mirror of the bathroom and fix my long curly hair as I glance at my almond eyes then the corners of my lips, lifted slightly towards the sky; unlike my mom's, whose weighted energy has somehow pulled them down to the dark earth.

My grandma's old mustang is rumbling outside, and my sister, brother and I race to the car like we are going to Disney Land. Us kids hop in the back seat, and we are headed to the other side of the tracks.

...

The house is small with blue walls and extremely clean and new. Pictures of a family with dark features and brown skin hang on the living room walls in fancy frames. A long table sits in back with what looks like covered trays of food. A microphone and podium stand in front of folded-out chairs with people sitting in them. All eyes look our way.

Immediately an old Philippine man greets us with a warm smile and shakes my mom's and dad's hands. Our matriarch mom's face is still stone cold.

"Come on kids," my mom motions us to sit down after the man shakes all of our hands with his warm palms cupping ours. I look down shyly and see my brother with his face already to the ground. We all sit in the very last row, except my dad who is standing in the back. I don't ask why.

A shorter man with a suit and tie comes up to us and shakes my mom's hand too.

"Hi, I'm Pastor Joe," he says with his child-like smile.

"Leah," my mom says in a low tone.

"Are these your kids?"

"Yes," she answers bluntly.

"What's your name?" He reaches his hand out to my brother. My brother looks down again and puts out his hand.

"Jason," my brother says under his breath.

"Hi Jason, welcome. So glad to have you guys on this Sunday morning."

He gets my sister's and my name, and my heart rate has begun to speed up and I feel a shaking in my hands. I glance at my mom's hands and see they are fidgeting too. I've always noticed my mom's hands don't stop moving. Even while steering a car they just keep dancing on the wheel, but I don't question it like I don't question what I've heard of my mom. I just look straight ahead as soothing music has begun to play with the old man's guitar strings, and the people in folded-out chairs begin to sing in unison.

My brother begins to giggle, but I look straight ahead at the pastor who is singing loudly and raising his hands with palms faced outward as if he is surrendering to something in the sky. Almost everyone in the crowd is doing the same, but my mom is looking straight with a focus I've never seen before.

Suddenly, I see her begin to open her mouth as if she is whispering the lyrics that everyone else is belting. I once heard from my oldest sister that my mom used to sing often in bars. She said she had a beautiful voice; and that people said she sang from the heart. They'd come just to hear her sing in bars in the '60s and '70s: a time and space much different than this 90's house-made-chapel, I'm sure. The music has trailed off and the pastor reaches out to grab his big black bible. He sets it on the podium in front of him and the room silences as if waiting on him to say something that will wow a crowd. I wait anxiously for what will happen next. My mom has her hands on her lap and her fingers are still dancing, and I can't decide if it is because of her anxiety - like me - or effects of some poison thing running through her body.

None of us have bibles. Another older man comes up to my mom with a big burgundy one and my mom reaches up slowly and takes it.

I am sitting by my mom and she opens it to a page in the New King James version that says John at the top.

"And the Word was with God and the Word was God," I hear the trailing words of the pastor at the podium.

My mom is looking down at the gold-trimmed book in front of her. I see her wipe her eye and I realize she has just shed a tear.

She looks again at the book that seems to have reached and pulled something out of her and sniffles. I've never seen my mom cry. Her face is either frozen or faintly smiling at me. But at this moment, I feel a small flutter inside as my mom clears her throat.

"Everyone, bow your head and close your eyes." The pastor instructs us, gently. "If anyone would like to accept Jesus into their hearts, raise your hand."

I sit there with my hands on my lap like my mom and my eyes partly closed because I don't know what this means.

The room is still as if waiting on something like a voice to speak from the sky. I look up and no one has raised hands as shy kids in a classroom, but I feel my stomach begin to rise to my throat. The room is still mute, and heads still bowed, and the voice has not called from the sky yet.

We wait a moment more like waiting for water to boil. I feel something stirring as if it will begin forming bubbles at any moment.

That's when I see - from the corner of my eye - my mom's hand raise slowly in the calm air, and it feels like a whisper has just hushed the room. Her head is still bowed, and now she is wiping tears away quickly as they come.

The pastor immediately walks up to her along with the old man and an old woman with a knee-length skirt on. The old man touches her shoulder and the pastor her forehead, and soon the whole congregation has hands pointed toward her.

My mom begins weeping as if she has not cried in years. She gasps every two seconds, and the butterflies in my heart begin to flutter their wings.

I wonder what will come next.

After the service, my brother, sister and I go to the long table to get plates the old man hands us, and we fill them up with strange food we have never eaten.

I sit down with them as my brother makes a joke, and my sister cackles and I giggle. The atmosphere has shifted to warmth, and it is like that fearful thing in the air has evaporated as the room fills up with more movement and laughter. I turn my head to see my mom still wiping tears away as the pastor is talking to her. Her eyes glance my way and she smiles a soft smile, and the butterflies still flutter their wings.

Stability

The stability of a home
Is always lit in the rooms of my mind
It settles as the house creaks
The quiet sound of breath deep
A place to rest
These rooms
Once
The earth quaking eruption
Of a girl's spirit grumbling
Chaotic
The aftermath of a building falling
Like the screaming scattering people
Of my mind
Chaotic
As the house of rage not refuge
Fueled by two friction sticks
A mother
A father
Drug addicts
The only home I know
Stability is a word I so savor
Sticks to my tongue like sweet candy
Or the cookies a mother bakes
To warm a heatless home
The kind of stability I have bent knee for
Picked up shattered glass for
Pieced brokenness back together
For
Stability
In the stables of my mind

Bob Dylan

Bob Dylan's voice was always blaring in the background of our dark home as my mom sang along with the monotone musician. My mom never talked much, but always seemed to muster up the vocals for belting Bob Dylan's lyrics - her favorite musician from her hippie days until then. Us kids would just walk in the door from playing some game of hide-and-seek or hopscotch in our neighborhood of boomboxes and rap beats. But my mom seemed to always disappear into the backroom like she was hiding something from us seekers. Bob Dylan's songs continued to play on repeat.

...

I guess an inkling of me always knew it was strange for my mom to sing ferociously a 1960s rock musician's songs in the middle of an urban hood at a time when rap music was emerging. The kids on my block would throw jabs at her, saying, "your mom is weird," or "why is your mom listening to that country music?" I would just laugh it off, having no real explanation for her bazaar behavior. She was my mom – the same bushy-haired, bra-less, moccasin-wearing mom I always knew.

The feeling of never really knowing her surfaced the time I found my sister and cousin sharing secrets of her in our bedroom. They revealed it like they were uncovering something illegal - that only they knew about - and now I was welcomed into forbidden territory. The secret was like access to an unknown world - to an unknown truth: like a young kid understanding Bob Dylan's songs that string along in a most sorrowful hymnal. His lyrics sang like poetry from out of some deep, mournful soul my mom clearly understood - possibly as much as her own.

Truth is like the light. It can expose and reveal things hidden in the depths of our hearts; but the revelation can sometimes come too soon. I was twelve years old when I was able to understand that my mom had a drug addiction. It was talked about behind closed doors, in secret closets, but never out in the open. We hid it away like skeletons in a closet. We hid it away like my mom hid in a dark room – locked away, forbidden.

...

I was nine years old and in a dark closet with the door closed tightly. A stream of light seeped through showing my toes curled up so they might not be exposed to passersby. I felt the jokester in me form a smile as I heard my mom calling my name from the kitchen and then from the hall, and then from my room. But I stayed still and quiet.

At that moment, I wanted them to miss me. I wanted *her* to miss me.

"Call grandma," my sister says. "She might have walked over there."

Finally, I heard my mom sobbing like something just died. That's when I came out.

"I'm right here," I said, feeling like my joke had gone too far.

My mom just hugged me tightly, wiping away her tears.

"Don't do that again," she says softly. "You scared me, sweetheart."

...

I was 12 years old when my dad came to live with us after years had passed and I had become a quiet, reserved pre-teen with suppressed emotions. He drank as often as a bottle was near. He, too, was something of a hippie in the 60's and 70's. His favorite musicians were the Beatles, whom he listened to as much as he drank brown whiskey from the bottle.

But my mom changed when he came to live with us. At first, she smiled. Then smile turned to scowl every time he tried to be a disciplinary father. Soon, bad words were spit up like fire from inside a deep volcano that had finally erupted after years of brewing and bubbling.

On a day like no other, the fire-cracking pops had become an overflow as blows were thrown and my brother, sister and I hid away in a backroom. We peeked out and saw an old-school dial phone thrown like a heavy brick at the speed of lightning. They were hollering blood and murder as we remained as mice in a room with the door locked. Outside, secrets were being revealed in the form of deep-seated hatred and blame. I felt my heart pounding and fumes rising inside myself; but I remained behind the door, as fear has a way of paralyzing.

We often fear shedding light on our mistakes because it is shameful; even when the music of life plays a melody that echoes our reality.

But, try as we might, the truth has a way of erupting and surfacing those things concealed in our hearts.

...

The next day, we were in the small home church and my dad remained in the back of the home, standing and leaning against the wall, while my mom and us kids sat down in the back row. We all watched as the guitar man strummed the cords, and the congregation opened up palms like they were giving up something to the heavens. It was as if they had just shed cloaks, and now they were presenting themselves naked in front of some deity by way of revelatory worship songs.

That day, it was as if the music shook something beneath the surface of time and space, and the rock bottom of life when my mom accepted the invitation of confession and something like a new heart. At that same moment in time, I heard the door in the back of us creak open and close. I turned to the window my dad was facing and saw him walking away from the house. Soon he vanished from sight. Sometimes, revelations just come too soon.

I wouldn't hear Bob Dylan's sorrowful tune stream from my mom's stereo system again after that.

Later, we'd sit in a brightly lit kitchen with the back door open as Christian worship music played from her CD player, and I'd feel a piece of heaven float between its walls like we were in that small home church again.

She'd tell me she was only trying to protect us kids.

And I'll say, "I know."

Seven years later…

II
Runaway

Run Away

Run away with me he said
With closed lips and soft eyes
Piercing through me
But I read his mind
Runaway –
To higher places, like the plane traces
In the sky
We'll ride high –
You'll be like that girl envied
With your arm around mine

Your head held high
Now that you have me
You'll be just fine
Through his dark brown eyes
I saw the blue skies
And the sun shined brighter as we sat in the darkness
That surrounded us
His dark hand caressing my thighs
And his lips
With the bitterness
Of Hennessy touching mine
I ran away with him
I ran away with him to better days, in a haze
I ran away with him, as my spine tingled, and our bodies tangled
I ran away with him as his warmth touched my cold
His eyes now closed
No longer revealing the light
I ran away with him
And as the fogginess faded from my brain the next day
And as my eyes tried to adjust to the light
I realized he had run away.
Left did he, the darkness though,
Still surrounding me
Now alone.
Run away with me he said,
But then again, maybe he did not
Maybe I ran away, in a blur,
Now with blurry eyes, and shaky limbs
On the ground now
How do I stand now?
I Ran away
Toward a promise he did not say,
I ran away,
In darkness now I stayed
And on this ground, I lay,
Unable to move at all
Nor stand tall
I ran away with a man I never knew,

And eyes I never read,
On this ground
I lay my bed
I'm a runaway
Instead

Year 2001

No sky is clearer than the day you are released from a mental institution.

My mom has my bag in her hands as I stroll behind her on a day when the radiant sun in the crystal-blue sky is the highest. Birds fly overhead as my mom unlocks the passenger door of her car and I get in.

"How was it there?" She asks.

I try to conjure up memories I cannot recollect. The first thing was going there that is a blur of suicidal attempt, and a dark hospital room and a woman in a white coat. The second thing was the darkness of sleeping for four days straight. Too tired to wake up to life. Facing reality was something like facing shame, guilt and a hospital bed I would rather not be in. They closed the blinds twenty-four seven while I lay there like a mummy. I never knew if it was day or night; sunny or overcast.

"It was fine." I lie.

She just stays quiet. I told my mom I took a handful of pills four days ago, but I never told her why. I guess I didn't know at the time. I just knew I was in a dark place. Dark because he didn't talk to me anymore. Darker because no matter how hard I tried I could never seem to find happiness. She blames school and pressure. I blame myself.

He really was a nice guy. His dreadlocks hung over his yellow-brown face and his hat turned sideways made him cool when he introduced himself the day of our coffee shop orientation. We strolled side-by-side at the Sacramento river on a summer's evening as he talked about his plans of touring in his breakdance crew – flying off to Europe and Japan. He said he wanted to take me there. I laughed in the cool night air thinking about how good that sounded; thinking about how that would probably never happen.

He dropped me off back home and I closed the wood door. Later that night, I'd open it again and go out with another guy I met at school that day.

...

"You knew I cared about you," he said under his breath while we were on the phone. I am in the middle of my room as tears are welling up in my eyes as he says he wants nothing to do with me.

He hangs up the phone, and I sit there because I have nowhere to go and no one to confide in. A silent tear drops from my eye as I feel my heart shattering before me, and I am tired. I crawl into my bed in the middle of a summer's day and won't wake up again until night when everything seems to crumble, and pills are swallowed down. And everything turns dark.

...

It's such a strange feeling being in a hospital room because you're alive, but you feel mostly dead. Death, of what I can tell, is strange that way. You are separated from life and people. The sterile hospital reminds me of that detachment. It reminds me of the loneliness and the dark outer space – out of space and time. And when you are out of space and time it must mean death. The hospital is the closest thing to death I know. Patients gasping for air; some yelling from pain. But for me – I stayed out of space and time – alone. And the strangeness of loneliness perhaps is the exact reason it feels so strange – because we are not meant to be there. In essence, it is death – the death of a heart.

...

The drive home is a solemn one. I sit thinking about my decision of dating too many young men. I think about the hurt I've caused – the hurt of a friend, the hurt of myself. And I wonder if I will ever find my way back to healing.

We arrive home.

School is in a couple of hours, but my mom asks if I'm going to stay home.

"No, I'm okay," I tell her and go into my room to get ready.

I put my bag of clothes on the floor of my cluttered room.

The room is the same. The bed still unmade, the dresser drawers partly cracked, and the window curtain still hides blinds where soft sunlight is shedding through.

I sit on my bed. My mind drifts to him and his glum-tone and how I treated him.

I glance at my notebook of poetry no one has ever read and pick it up. I turn to a blank page and the pen begins to pour eloquent words of apology. A warm tear trickles from my eye and drops onto the lined paper and I hope it doesn't bleed.

"I know it doesn't mean anything now," I write. "But I'm sorry."

When I finish spilling my true feelings like blood onto paper, I fold it up, grab my purse and fly out to my car.

The air outside is warm and fresh, and above is a cloudless sky of blue. I feel something like the sun in my chest beam like horizons, and I am hopeful of new beginnings.

I drive as the trees ruffle in the soft breeze and see sun rays light up buildings overhead. I think about school and my mom and everything I have and what I almost gave up.

I roll up to the coffee shop with my letter in my shaky hand and get out of the car. He is at the register and my hands have become uncontrollable as a seizure. He looks up and glares at me from across the counter. I step up, reach out my hand with the letter inside and he slowly takes it. He smiles and I smile back.

He once said I never open up. Well, here was my chance at breaking the ice.

"Thanks," he says and goes to the back while I order a drink.

When he reappears, he is smiling gleefully as if I have just given him everything he's ever wanted.

"I'll come get you after I get off, okay? We'll go somewhere," he says.

"Okay," I say with a smile and push the door open to walk out to my car sitting under the summer's sun. I feel something like a weight has been lifted and somehow see a piece of my heart again. And the day never looked so clear.

Parted

The heavens parted for me
The sky
Parted clouds
The shape of smoky mountaintops
Opened my eyes to God-like light
A patch of white
The color of new linen
Or
Wedding-gown lace
In the darkest of days
A sign
For a girl
Driving on an empty road
Rain
Pit patters on a window shield
A heart
Beating the sound of brokenness
The pain of the tearing apart
Two dark pasts now on different paths
He may float away
But she
She will climb
The cloudy mountain
She has seen it with her own eyes
On a trip somewhere close to the sky
Get lost somewhere
Somewhere
Anywhere
But here
Where haze covers visions of growth
Green trees of new beginnings
Lost
Like the girl driving aimlessly in a storm
Thoughts

Stems of him
Breaking off in her mind
Tears as many –
As the unforgiving rain
Lost
Not knowing when she'll begin again
But then
The sky
Parts for her
To see
The dark may cover for a time
But
As the universe
May have it
The sun
Always
Appears
Again

The Death of Age

The music dances in my ear
The sound
Of every sad ballad I have ever heard
Strings along
Beethoven and Mozart
From some foreign old age
On a tape cassette player in my room
As I listen to past and present
Join together like dancing partners
I will unlearn my age
With music from past lives
I will become in fact a past life
An old soul
An old woman
A Mute
Dancing in a dark room
To the music of him
And I
As I reach into past
To grab ghost of him into
Present
I will dance in the moonlit night
With the death of us
Play the piano and flute
Of funeral
Over and over again
Until tears run dry
And I
Dance in to
Dawn of a new day

Clean

Her eyes have become my dirty windows
The outside panes too stained for strength
Cleaning her means cleansing her
She has become the soil in my soul
We stand
Face to face
I often look the other way
Or to the back of her
A bathroom door
I will open again
The foreign door to sin
He will be waiting wondering where I am
Wandering his mind
To a tossed bed
Then the act
That tingles the body
The only reason for the invitation
Smear his name with permeating ink all over
A body
For A moment in time
The clock on the wall seems to have stopped
Time standing still as my hands on this sink
As I turn to look in the mirror
Past, present and future seem all to be here
Surrounding me like a circle of counsel
Tells me if I go out there
I will become the cycle of this drug
I have the needle of my eye
Halfway to my vein
I see
All tainted window
The raindrop tears only partly remove

It is the hands and arms that do the work
There is a day
I will wipe away
The grime of him
And them
And then, I will begin to see her again

III

Joseph Dreams

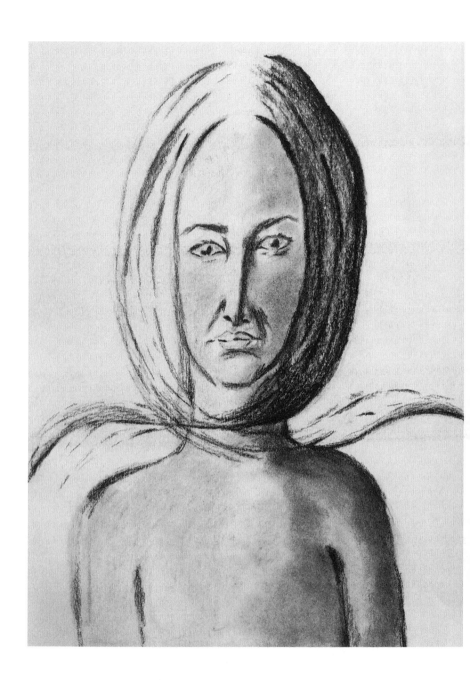

Joseph Dreams

I lost the key to these thoughts I can't unlock
My mind was a prison cell - I yell, forget to talk
I swear he hears me from heaven's lofty heights
If I scream blood and murder think he'll open those gates?
My youth was angel wings and butterfly bellies
My woman was demon eyes and beautiful bird killings
Still I remember the pews of you and I
As we dance in the river of peace and joy
But as we sit in the presence of laments and cries
I know fire burns our circle, but we have to try
If we close our eyes and Joseph-dream again
I think I might just fly like that feather-bird to the wind
Dance a little longer in the river and wade
Heaven might just be a mile away

Year 2003

I'm standing in the middle pew listening to the worship team's rising and falling notes like angels bowing down before God in heaven. I listen as the guitar strums and the piano prances and the tambourine jingles, and I am in heaven. The woman in front and center is belting out the lyrics like she is calling on God to come down from his throne and present himself before the thirty-something members in the room. My hands rise, and my voice quietly sings the notes I have memorized in my mind because for two years my mom and I have attended this church and the songs have not changed. My mom is at my side, and I hear her strong voice rise and fall with the worship team, and the whole congregation sings in unison like we are those angels in heaven rising and falling.

...

Before that church, we went to a church right down the street from where we lived: in that poor district with many jobless mothers and fatherless kids. We'd walk down the gritty street as tree branches swung overhead during the spring and summer months trailing up to the double doors of a church building my mom found her heart in. It was in that church that my mom found purpose: singing in a church choir and prayer.

There, my mom sat with eyes fixed in the front row, while us kids were in the back joking about church members and writing silly notes to pass the time as the pastor preached salvation to a community suffering from poverty and lack of true guidance. I pretended not to listen like the rest of the kids, but later that night I'd think about what the pastor preached and flip open a hardcover journal, and write poetry and dreams to a God I only hoped was listening. A God whom my mom sang and talked to every night in the form of whispers and closed eyelids and a face pointed towards heaven.

I was always searching for something greater than myself. Something in my young heart wanted purpose like my mom. So, I was always looking to heaven for an answer; especially after the dating escapades when redemption seemed so near. Even so, I could never seem to see my way passed tears of never feeling like enough.

...

Fasting is like forcing yourself to be stretched and pulled by one of those Midi-evil tormenting machines. At least that is what I think because I have not eaten in a week in a half and have only drunk measly water morning, noon and night and I am tired.

The church fasted for a couple of days but ate hefty meals every night in an attempt to get an answer from God. Me – I fast for an answer too, but I have no question. I just do it because I feel I should be the best Christian, but my thin sweater has gotten baggy, and my pants are hanging off my hipbones and I am tired. However, I keep going because I want to make it to two weeks as I told myself.

They say Christianity is enduring hardship. This not eating is hard. I watch as my family eats hardy dinners of tacos my mom has fried up and ice cream they indulge in, but I won't give in. I just sit there as saliva wets my tongue, and I am like a puppy watching humans eat food I cannot have. But I won't give in.

My mom is asking when I am going to be done fasting and I tell her when God speaks to my heart. She just looks at me with deep-concerned eyes then puts her head down to the bible on her lap. And I go back into my room alone and lay on my bed and listen to the growling in my stomach. And I am tired.

...

It's Thursday, and I have vowed Sunday, the Sabbath, I would stop fasting. But hunger has gotten the best of me, and I rip open the can of cashews by my bedside and begin devouring them like they are milk and honey from the Promised Land. Their sweet, salty flavor soothes my taste buds, and the watering in my mouth ceases and at this moment they are the best food I have ever eaten.

After I gorge myself on cashews, I feel a profound disappointment in myself like I have let God down. I feel the shame of my decision to not honor my word and keep the hunger going until the Sabbath. I lay on my bed with a full stomach and stare at the pearly - white ceiling as my heart sinks with regret.

...

I'm sitting in the third pew again, and it is Sunday. My mom is at my side with her hands lifted high singing in her deep-pitch tone, and I sing with a head bowed under my breath. My hands are raised slightly, and the music sings something about God's love. Tears welt in my eyes and one slips out and falls down my cheek and onto the flat carpet of that old church floor. Another one drops onto it like it is going to make a stain, and now I have stained my cheeks with tears.

The pastor walks up to the podium. He is a white man in his mid-forties - not like the older pastor in our old church. But, his message - just like the other - is clear as crystal to me: that God loves us even though we fail as people. I think about my fasting and how I've failed.

Then he says something about love, and I think about love and I have moved to tears again.

After the congregation has gone their separate ways, and my mom and me are in her old Toyota Corolla, she asks if I want to go get something to eat at a restaurant. I say yes.

We drive down the two- way road as the streets blur and the trees swing overhead like in my youth, and I remember the word love.

And somehow the line between love and ritual has blurred like my vision through tears.

We pull up to IHOP and my mom meets me at the front of the car. She wraps her arm around mine and pulls open one of the double doors for me to walk through.

We sit by a window as the white light streams on my mom's dark-almond eyes, and her Mexican face has become a shade or two lighter. I gobble down pancakes with strawberry syrup and gulp down the orange juice and glance up at my mom. Her eyes are looking into mine like they could just be the eyes of heaven. She is smiling softly as the light that is shedding on her. Suddenly, it is like a weight has been lifted from my chest. I pick up the fork again and feel the gooey syrup warm my taste buds and the rumbles of my hollow stomach quiet.

Miracle

Young woman once cried bitter tears under suffocated sheets
Begging maker grant miracle so she can just breathe
A hole of depression has filled these lungs
It boils up and spews out sourness from the tongue
She says life is all numbness and pain
But she knows the sun will shed rays again
Light her eyes as lightning fills the sky
Pours showers of pain but God will not forget me
Shakes covers off and plants feet on cold ground
Depression is colder, but warmth of a promise she's found
Some whispers in her spirit let her know she's still breathing
And can walk every day, so these limbs still have feeling
The miracle is the walk, the pushing forward daily
The backbone of overcoming falling and failing

Two years later…

IV
Rock Bottom

Rock Bottom

I am everything of gritty streets of my past
I am nothing of golden spoons paving of cash
It's hardship and toil expending my royal hues
I've never been given anything but prayers I presume
But hands intertwined to the infinite sky
Lifted my spirits from under heavy clouds and I -
Being poor as the beggar on the street -
Continue to follow trails to well of fortune in me
I'm just a girl with fists-clenched to whispers of prayer
On bloody knees as mind bleeds the color of insanity
Drip dropping on the pavement of you and me
A foundation of flowers growing through crooked cracks
The miracle of life lies at rock bottom in fact -
If you look up, you'll see gold suns and crystal skies
Wipe tears away because something has stopped these cries
Pushing and panting for air has lifted this load
And joy has been given from seeds planted and sewed

Year 2005

I'm sitting on a floral couch in my mother's home in the early winter months, slumped over and sinking further into a deep, coma-like sleep. After the third hospital, Depakote was the highest form of antipsychotic medication the doctor prescribed to keep me static and sitting still: to still the voices in a mind that landed me in Schmick Mental Health Treatment Center in Downtown Sacramento. It was one of the three institutions I visited the year of 2004 - the year they diagnosed me bipolar and schizophrenic all at once.

"She'll never be the same again," the psychiatrist at U.C. Davis Medical Center downtown tells my mom the day after my release. I'm sitting next to her makeup-less and broken out with ratted hair I have not washed in days.

"You might see some progress, but she'll never be like she used to be. So, you just have to take it day by day."

"I do not receive those words!" My mom yells, taking my limp hand as I spew out jumbled words that do not make sense. "My daughter will be healed in the name of Jesus!"

The doctor just looks at me with blue-pitied eyes the color of a salt-water ocean of tears.

My mom is a Christian and prays twenty-four seven. I never knew her prayers but every night she sleeps on a sleeping bag in the living room as she has for years. Her head tilts toward the ceiling and she whispers prayers under her breath. I know they are prayers because she tells me when I try to wake her. She's been a prayer warrior from the time we entered a small home church in South Sacramento until now. These days, I know she is praying for me as the days have turned dark and cold and salvation has become the epitome of sanity.

...

My mom had picked me up from the last hospital after Christmas came and went. Throughout my stay, I had gained thirty pounds as a result of overeating fatty foods the doctors prescribed to the anorexic girl. They made sure the chefs served large portions to the mentally ill patient - a girl who fasted religiously for a year and a half. When I arrived at the hospital, I was cripple-weak and skeletal – double zero jeans hanging off my hip bones and a gaunt face to show my decaying, feeble body becoming dangerously cold by the day. The first hospital visit, they tied my comatose body to a bed, strapped my arms with fluid-filled tubes and waited for the unconscious girl to wake up from deep sleep: dark as the arctic ocean my mind was swallowed up into. A mother weeping silently at my side touched my iceberg hand and whispered prayers under her breath I could not make out.

But here, in my mother's house, I sit, submerged into a couch of faded pink flowers the same as the matching loveseat across from me my mom sits on - the same woman listening to me babble about my detest for being in this foreign body. Memories in my head float like dead fish in water of a thin, petite girl. I was the girl guys once peered at with gawking eyes. I was the light-hearted, smiling girl in the mirror – a girl to be envied.

But that smile has faded into the background along with those couch-flowers, the body I long for, and that weightless heart.

"How am I going to ever lose weight if I keep eating!" I ask my mom who is looking at me with distressed, almond brown eyes – the ones I reflect. But mine have become black as a dark tunnel and unrecognizable. After the last hospital - St. Helena– any ounce of joy I had was left there in Napa Valley, along with feasts that brought about the nostalgia of home. A thick layer of depression had managed to blanket my senses – and, as a result, the numbness has become my existence. I am jobless, broke and have reached rock bottom. And hope I had for a new beginning when I returned has now disintegrated into the earth of dirt and grime – soon to be buried like bodies, forever.

"You'll lose it," she says in a whisper.

"I can't. I keep eating. I'll never be like I was before!"

My mom just sits there, nodding her head as hollers of loathing filter the air of our small, Victorian home - filling the life-vacant abode. Bitter words the taste of rotten fruit stem from my mouth and string along as days turn into weeks and weeks into months - repeating the same disturbing vibrations.

...

When my mom is at work, I sit in front of a motionless TV - blank as my stare. I don't turn it on because I have lost interest and gained lethargy. Taking steps seems a daunting task. Dirty dishes are beginning to pile up in the small kitchen, and dust on the window blinds is settling, making its abode in seal crevices. Lifelessness has gotten the best of me and waiting for my mom to walk through the door is becoming my detested existence.

"When am I going to lose weight!" I yell on no particular winter's day. The winter days in Sacramento vary often from overcast as ocean fog to clear as blue waters. These days they are bright, cold and clear. I see the fresh dew of the morning melting by a winter's sun, but I don't feel it. It's like my heart is listless, my body senseless, and my mind unclear as dark, muddy waters. I see nothing in the future. I see only past in bits and pieces like flashes of a movie, never transposing the full film for me to reflect on how I got here. Fragmented thoughts interrupt seamless ones, and I am left with sitting and waiting on brokenness to be mended.

My mom comes home to find me at my usual post – sunken into a floral couch of faded flowers as the ones that have gone dormant on our porch. In my foggy vision of a living room, I have been sitting and waiting for her. My eyes look up into hers and, at this moment, I am reminded of my downcast appearance. My mom's angelic face reflects the demon in me, and, in turn, my heart has grown sour. It spills over like my gut over my now tight-fitting bell-bottom jeans. My shirt has become too small, showing two layers of belly that just keep growing, and I am sitting on an ever-expanding derrière.

"It'll happen, sweetheart," my mom says in her slow, quiet tone of solace. "I know it's hard. But you'll see. Everything has a shelf life."

My mom has said this phrase several times and I wonder what it means. A shelf is where cups and bowls are placed like in the small white cupboards of my mom's quaint home. We don't have too many, but they sit there until their time comes to drink or eat out of them – as I now do so often.

My mom makes steak and potatoes, and tacos are a favorite. It's just my mom and me in her house most of the time and we eat dinner solemnly until I begin unleashing the beast of misery within. And the shelf time seems to never end.

We transition into the living room after dinner where pictures of all four of us kids sit in the built-in shelves, but I don't see them in person too much anymore. Since my illness, our hearts have grown apart and it's just my mom and me – eating together, sitting together, and waiting together.

I tell my mom again and again that I will never be normal, nor her healing prophecy ever come into fruition. My mom tells me it's not true; I will be healed. I tell her I'm miserable. She tells me it won't last forever.

"You'll see," she says.

...

At another checkup with my psychiatrist in the same stale, white-walled room, the doctor asks how the Depakote medication is working. She is scribbling notes on the lined paper I cannot make out. Not because I cannot see them, but because my mind has lost the ability to focus and reading is like piecing together a hundred-piece puzzle.

"I hate the way I look," I blurt out because I now work solely on impulse. "I can't fit into any of my clothes. I can't stop eating." I give her the answer to her question in the form of a 140-pound girl who thinks that if she drops to 110, she will be normal.

"I know it's frustrating, but is the medication helping your depression?"

"I guess," I lie. At this moment in time, I feel nothing but sluggishness that happens after the draining of a body twisted like a soppy dishrag - now shriveled up and dry.

She tells me there is a new medication called Abilify and most people lose weight on it. I tell her I want to try it.

"It's going to take time for adjustment," she says, but I don't care.

"I want to look like I did before."

...

My mom and I sit on the stained green and pink floral couch and loveseat across from each other on a spring's day after four powdery pills are prescribed, and I start taking them religiously every night the way my mom says her prayers on the wooden floor.

My mom and I used to go to the church across town. We did it for two years during my depression. We sat in the middle pew next to one another, listening to the middle-aged white pastor preach about living as a good Christian. The church has become a bad memory, and my mom and I have stopped going due to the mental illness that somehow has managed to keep me away from life, people and feeling.

Tonight, I miss the days of worship music playing from the band on the platform of that small church. I miss my mom's deep, passionate singing and my fluttering heart. I miss the quietness of prayer and the goodness of the girl I used to be before fasting escapades got the best of me.

Tonight, the winds have shifted, and the seasons changed, although the floral couch remains the same – in a standstill position where my mom and I sit as we have for days on end.

I get up as I feel something like venom arise in my throat as voices become unrestrained like a python in my mind. I lash out - my fist into the air of the grim night, striking it against a stiff white wall, hoping to tear flesh and breakthrough skin to show physically what I feel in my soul. I want to create a hole in walls that cannot seal screams of agony, but my screams do not restrain the python, rather they exacerbate it.

"I hate God!" I scream. "All he wants to do is make me suffer!"

My mom just sits on the couch with legs crossed and troubled eyes looking straight ahead in a Victorian home that offers no answers from mute white walls. Her tattered bible is on her lap, opened to one of those pages from the New King James version, but she does not say the words out loud when she glances toward the gold-trimmed page. I see her moving lips, but I doubt she is reading silently. Rather, she is praying.

My mom finally yells back after my voice has gone hoarse and throat raw. "God is helping you carry this cross!" She says as if fighting me in a war of the hearts – a battle she is losing every day. I'm digressing, and this fit of hysteria is nearly unbearable for me.

I sit down after I find that I cannot break through the wall even after all of my attempts of punching through it. My knuckles are welt and fingers barely extend now. I am tired and have worn myself out enough to finally fall asleep.

I plop down on the couch across from my mom.

I see my mom begin to get teary-eyed, and she wipes a gliding tear away from her Mexican-brown cheek. I return to her a scowl because my senses have run dry, and I cannot seem to cry.

I just sit there as misery occupies space in my heart.

That's when she begins to tell me:

"I know how you feel," she says. "Because the same thing happened to me." She is now weeping. "After I stopped taking drugs, I went insane."

She tells me she screamed into a pillow in the dead of night while us kids were asleep in an attempt to seal her howls of agony - secretly hoping no one would find out and take us kids away from her.

My mom took drugs when we were younger. She'd hide behind a closed door in our eerie-dark house where she barely turned on lights. We were too young to notice. Later, I'd find out she, neighbors and siblings used that room to get high while us kids played outside in the summer sun, distracted by child-like amusement. Right when my mom got her welfare check, she'd disappear. But when she came home, she'd have groceries in her hand and soon tacos cooked. She tried.

Now she cooks a meal every night for me after time has passed and seasons have changed, and she finds what joy she can in the simple things – like cooking or watering flowers on the porch.

"I know why it happened to me – because I took drugs. I just don't know why this had to happen to you," she says between pants of breath.

"I used to curse God too," she says, while tearstains glisten on her full cheeks. "But God helped me out of that. And he'll help you too."

I can't seem to care or share empathy for her. I can't seem to conjure up feelings that people feel when other people are shedding skins and shedding tears. I only sit in the pit of anguish and scream my final scream into the air of the grim night before I crawl on a floral couch to go to sleep, hoping God hears me and changes my universe.

...

My mom and I drive my small 1991 Toyota Corolla to a specialty furniture store across town. It looks like summer outside although it is still a month in spring. We go inside and peer at all of the furniture made for houses with luxury furniture – not like my mom's small house of hand-me-down furniture and dusty table lamps.

We walk down isles and I stare at furniture that has become uncomfortable and spending money unstimulating.

That's until one catches my eye - a full-body mirror with fancy-black detailed borders – the most expensive one in the store.

"Let me buy that for you," my mom says and looks at me with a hopeful smile the shape of a child's innocence. I know she is hoping it will bring me some joy.

I say okay, and we walk the cumbersome mirror up to the register to ring up my new gift.

...

I look into the mirror that sits at the foot of my unkempt bed every day and night. The background shows a room that hasn't been cleaned in months. The hamper is filled with dirty clothes I can't find the strength to clean, and dust is beginning to settle on the tarnished lamp by my bedside. My energy is still depleted, but the effects of Abilify seem to be working as I see the reflection of a girl shrinking almost daily thanks to the new medication and my mom who has stopped making tacos for us and has transitioned to chicken salads and sandwiches.

I hang onto memories of a girl with glowing eyes, a petite frame, and a joyful heart. I hang onto this even as my mind becomes a tornado at night and I scream for it to stop. I hold tight as fists clinched to memory as if it could save me; as if it could be relived.

...

Sierra Vista Mental Healthcare Facility is a psychiatric institution that exists on the outskirts of Sacramento, tucked away in buildings you may pass by on any given day without noticing. It houses mentally ill patients and housed the most memorable of all of my stays in a psychiatric institution. It was there that I found joy I never had prior, stored in a mentally ill girl hidden away like that brick building cars pass by daily.

At that hospital, my mom came to visit me, bringing big trays of assorted cookies for all the patients. She always had a wide smile on her face and squeezed me tightly as her warm arms wrapped around my body, and suddenly, I was that cheerful girl again.

Excitement welt up in my chest every time I saw my mom as I'd spent two months away from her thus far – behind the doors of an institution that only allows one visit per day for one hour.

Maybe the happiness was because of the medication they prescribed there; maybe it was because I got out of a psychiatric bed; or maybe, it was because of my mom's joyful heart rubbing off on me, if but for a short time.

Later, I'll wonder where all that joy went and how to get it back.

...

Winter, spring, and summer have passed and fall leaves are beginning to turn their colors and fall to the gritty ground. My mom still showers her flowers even as the seasons have changed and the sun sets earlier. It's fall of 2005, and I still sleep on a faded floral couch of my mom's aged home.

This morning, I wake up to see the pale sun shed light through the dusty blinds and feel a stream of warmth touch my face. I see the light reflect on the coffee table in front of me. I don't hear anything but creaking and settling of our home like some mighty force has just shaken it and passed over. My mom has left for the day to work and I am alone in the still, quiet home. I look around at the pictures of all four of us kids on the indented shelves and I am reminded of the shelf life.

I sit up and rub my eyes feeling peace like calm waters after a raging storm, but I can't say where it has come from.

Later, when my mom comes through the door, I am sitting on the couch as usual. I smile at her because I feel my heart finally ease. She smiles her innocent, girlish smile back.

We transition to the wood table in our compact kitchen where she makes salads on a cutting board, dicing tomatoes and cucumbers and putting them in the bowls she gets down from the shelf. And the time has come for them to be used again.

We sit in silence together as soft light illuminates our dinner meeting through the kitchen blinds. I cross my thin legs under the table and begin taking tiny bites of lettuce leaves and chicken breast. I look out the window between the dusty blinds and see my mom's rose bushes on the backyard deck with fallen leaves, but they are not quite wilted yet.

I break through the silence to talk about God and healing again, but I don't scream or shout. I just wonder if by healing she meant a heart being healed. I don't ask. I just sit with my mom eating salad and hear only the settling of an old Victorian home in the background.

Her Eyes

I see the words in my mother's eyes before she speaks them
They look like every sweet almond that has ever flowered
They speak of light after darkness
We sit in a kitchen as the sun hits them
So perfectly
As her words of, "It won't always be this way"
Shine like sterling silver
Telling me tomorrow will come
Although I have the bitter taste of
Bad fruit on my tongue
These days I have become
Something like the fruit of my mother's womb
As we sit in a kitchen and I tell her
That my mind has become a leper
A hardened, ill disfigurement
That has furrowed my brows
And transformed my eyes into the shape of
A crazy horse
Unlike the tamed, softness of hers
They tell me of her sorrows
They tell me of her strengths
They tell me of my strengths
We are alike in many ways
Her past has become my present
As circle of life would have it
But she –
She was the first fruit to break it
A lineage of women who bare children
Who never see the ripened age of new beginnings
But for me -
Her eyes have become resurrection after night
A reason to fight
For tomorrow in her eyes

Feeling

I told her I couldn't feel
As we sit on two plastic chairs in the middle of June
Slurping mango Jamba Juice
The color of the evening sun
It casts shadows of two women on the cement
Before us
And I
Have become a shadow of myself
Life itself has become a memory
As she tells me I will feel one day
As the bittersweet taste runs down my throat
Her words
Of "I will"
And
"One day"
Hold life
But also strength
Attained only
By carrying something so heavy
You have lost even the ability
To feel
Somehow though
Her words have become
The setting sun
That has the power
To
Illuminate
Even
The darkness

War on A Hospital Bed

Eyes
Closed
Wrestles in the dark
To open
On a hospital bed

A war
Within
Fights
At the picket line
To keep the divide
Between mind and spirit
Between house and home
It is in the sleep
I have managed to keep
From breathing
From allowing air to enter these windows
The expansion of these lungs
That holds the beat of my heart
But
It is the dark
Weighing down the sun
Turning my home pitch black
To exist behind lids
That twitch
As the fight
Persists
Opening now
Means opening
My third eye
In the realm
Where both entities
War
For a land (the heart)
That controls the breath that moves

Breathing life into existence
Or
Disease
But when eyes open
Surely, they will see
The sun that always seems
To rise again

Punching Walls

Punching walls was always the hard part. Hard because the knuckles always welt and throbbed with every angry throw. Harder because no matter how many times I battered the brick-like wall, I could never quite hit hard enough to breakthrough. Similarly, I could never seem to break through this abominable mental illness. When you are in a prison of your mind, all you want to do is break free. So, the next best thing? A blow to the wall as a swinging iron hammer: my frustration built up enough to beat bricks until bloody fists. But it left no hole of escape - only me - battered and bruised.

My mom sat with legs crossed and arms folded listening and watching every assault the old Victorian wall took.

One swing, two swings, three swings.

"I hate this fucking life!" I screamed louder than the unceasing torment that would not restrain no matter how much of an uncontrollable beast I became.

The turbulent time was a result of my mind being strangled by bipolar illness's mighty grip. As a victim of brutality, explosive behavior is sure to be a result. Breathe, I could, but only by gasping for relief from the mental illness as suffocating and overpowering as it was.

It was on that grave night in December that they took me to a hospital where I would lay for one week going in and out of coherence – stepping in and out of reality. Now, reality had become the gory nightmare and the nightmare was a girl spinning out of control with every sun that died. Replaced by a risen full moon or not, darkness always seemed to overcome.

"I hate God!" I screamed loud enough for my mom to hear, loud enough for anyone with an ear to hear, and loud enough for a God beyond solid walls, beyond far-off stars, and beyond a bipolar universe to hear.

"It won't always be this way," my mom said softly as a feather upon the skin, as she always tried to soothe my inner wounds since I would not let her anoint my sore-bruised knuckles.

"When!" I let out a gut-wrenching scream into the deafness of the night. "It's never going to happen!" I wailed in bitter anger and heart-filled agony. The psychiatrist and every doctor gave me no hope of ever getting through this mental illness to the other side where a sane individual might exist and live a normal life - one where peace exists in the heart like slow breathing.

"Now! I'm believing right now!" She countered my fits of fury as my fight for breath continued.

"No, it's not!" Swing.

"It's never going to happen!" Another swing.

My mom and I share the same eyes, the same nose, and in many ways, the same mind. Like me, she once lost her sanity to darkness. But her darkness was repercussions of much drug abuse. And mine – well it was a mystery – one filled with solitude and unjustified misery.

She sat on the floral couch of once-vivid colors staring into far-off space. She glanced up at me - the source of her aloofness - every time I said I hated God.

"God is helping you!" She pressed against my lashes as if fighting me in a match. I was digressing and fits of rage were my demise.

My mom is a Christian, whose faith has taken her from the depths of the darkness of drug addiction to a simple life where her focus is solely her kids' salvation. That is, in fact, *her* heart's song.

Just two months before, we rode in a car to church on the other side of town playing worship music as we did every Sunday, just her and I. And now, loneliness had become her entire world while I was away in mental incarceration; and that bible had become her only salvation, hanging on by a mere thread.

"God is helping you carry this cross," she told me, now in but a calm tone.

"No, he's not!" I said, striking the wall once again, and, once again, not even making the slightest dent in it.

"He doesn't care about me! All he wants is to make me suffer! I hate God!" Nothing could stop the insanity within – striking the same walls, hoping the result would be a breakthrough: a Christian's philosophy of obtaining a reward after a heart has persevered hardship.

It wasn't just the lack of control; it was the lack of feeling. At that moment in time, my heart was void of any type of joy, contentment or satisfaction that - on any given day - a person might feel. And the only thing I could feel was beating my flesh against what felt like prison gates - indefinitely binding me to a sentence I could not break.

"Everything has a shelf-time," my mom said, referring to seasons of life we go through and pages that turn for us all.

"You'll see," she said as a final word, and I would crawl onto a floral couch screaming my final heaving scream into the air of the night, hoping a God would hear my anger and change my heart.

Wounds

The wounds take longest to heal
Waiting
In a white-walled office
Watching
Hands touch numbers
That has become the focus of my eyes
Moves with them around the circle
Slow as my existence
I have become accustomed to this visit
A woman
Tells me of the clock standing still
As long as I am living
This illness will define my essence
I have become not a question mark
But a period
A blinking curser never moving
To type words, write my own story
Rather, the world has written me off
But the clock keeps ticking
Like this heart still beating
I have decided to keep living
Sitting
As open wounds gather air
But also fly in dust of
Frustration
Because everything moves with the wind
But I watch time
Waiting
On skin
To become cast
To become skin again
To become
Scar
A reminder of the splitting then the mending

The bleeding then the healing
The healing that takes away the pain

Strength

That thing that grows like wild thickets
In my veins
That thing
Reminds me of every IV tube
Attached to me
Injects me
With forced fluid
To keep my chest rising
And falling
The falling
Before the climbing
I will use these limbs for reaching
Then pulling
Up again and again
To keep myself from a bed
A needle
The feeble
Position of a body limp
The infant in me wants to scream
Because weakness has become the demon of me
I know that growth
Is a human being's destiny
That the pain of me
Will make me stronger
That bloodshed
Is power
Is honor
Is a nail piercing flesh
Brings back to life
The dead

Two months before the release…

Arms

He takes my arm; says he knew he would see me again
I have become a type of perpetual visitor,
As I enter doors - to many - a destiny
Greeted by name and eyes that have lost sensitivity
I on the other hand, don't see clearly
My sight has become impaired
This spinning wheel of thought has tossed me
And I
Have landed myself here again
In the arms of a closed building
A safe house for those who have lost the wheel
A collision I am all too familiar with
The walk through the halls is a dreaded one
I hear automated doors to the clearness of day
Closing in back of me
I don't say goodbye to the light in my mother's eyes
Rather turn to face the dark room ahead
The words he speaks from his puffed-up chest
For some reason
Don't demean me
Rather, they tell me
Of the many stories
He has seen replayed
Like a tragic movie
Or violent video game
I sense I have become a high number in his mind
The story at the top of his list
A statistic unspecified
But it is my name I fear
Spoken in a high-pitch sarcastic tone
That strikes me
That the girl with ratted hair
And makeup-less face
Coming through the narrow corridors
Is expected

Waited for even
It is my name greeted
With unfazed expression
And nonchalant gaze
And warm, welcoming arms
Grasped by the likeness of his
That keeps me from ever returning

Love Conquers

My mom and I sat on scratchy grey blankets between blank blue walls playing UNO. The room was silent since the girl I roomed with was still in the cafeteria eating the dry meatloaf and canned fruit. My seat next to her was empty since I had hurried to see my only visitor for the day. My mom.

Down the hall of open doors, we sat in number three. Right across from the open break room. Patients in pajamas passed us by looking in at my mom and me playing childish card games that lifted my heart like a child's balloon. I sat Indian style adjacent to her. She with her long, black curly hair and me with matching brown - twisted and turned into a French braid she braided whenever she visited.

The room smelled of old books and potpourri as we sat like two kids, carefree, playing cards between walls the color of my mood before they put me here, un-medicated. The nurse came in and gave me a paper cup with four pills and a small glass of water - a serving as a daily reminder of where we were. I took the small cup as my mom sat watching me with her hands still holding up three UNO cards. I tilted my head, quickly throwing the pills back then following with water to make sure they didn't get stuck on their way down: to be sure I did not get stuck in the second psychiatric institution I had spent two winter weeks thus far.

My mom put the card down, "UNO," she said, as the staff member left the room to my mom and me in our momentary sanctuary.

I let out a giggle.

"Again?" I said and she let out a high pitch laugh; the kind from your core that others turn to see and investigate where it came from. Then they'd smile themselves at the woman with deep creases in the corners of her mouth, a cheerful smile, and bright almond eyes - the color of kindness.

We sat on the bed like sitting on sands of an island when the lady watching my room peeked in and said, "Okay, Eliza, visiting is over."

My mom looked at me with the same eyes - deep as a bottomless ocean - every day they called time for visitors to leave their loved ones behind. Some patients had visitors; some had not. Those who had not spent visiting hours in the break room with a TV that played Disney movies on repeat. I never saw the girl in the bed next to me have a visitor come to see her.

We were allowed only one visitor once a day, and my mom was always promptly on time waiting at the door. Sometimes she'd miss her stringent job to see her daughter for one hour allowed: a door open for a short time to replay a card game like those juvenile Disney movies.

"Okay, I'll see you tomorrow," she said, kissing me on my cheek and wrapping her pillow-soft arms around me like a zipped puff-coat in the middle of a winter's cold.

"I love you, sweetheart," she said as we parted, and her warm hands still touched my arms. Then her deep-ocean eyes would get deeper, soon glossing over dark pupils.

"Love you," I said.

"Okay, bye Mija," she said, then tapped my arms, soon wiping away the ocean that spilled a salty stream over her cheeks.

I said goodbye, and my mom disappeared from the room leaving me alone behind the blue-walled room of "safety," as instructed by the psychiatrist. He had the supreme authority to do so, and my mom and I had no control over his decision.

But every day spent in that hospital where we sat on scratchy blankets playing a game of luck and chance my mom took hold of the one thing she had complete control over – love.

Blue Walls

There are blue walls in the rooms of my mind
Blank as canvass
Blue as sky
Surround me like the vast ocean
They tell me of the wide world
Ready to be painted with my footprints
But
I am in this place a stranger
On this island
There are many rooms here
With walls the same
As if we
Are the same
As if the same mental illness boat brought us here
But we are not the same
Some of us sleeping between those walls
Some of us looking at the walls
Some of us talking to those walls
And if these Walls could talk
They would tell you of all the manic,
Depressed, misunderstood people they house
But they will not tell you how they got there
That all their stories are different
And that the paths leading to these walls were never the same
But what they will tell you
Is that these beings have all seen
The blank canvass before them
Ready to be painted

Painted Freely

My oldest sister picked me up from the second psychiatric hospital on that gloomy winter day after the episodic wreckage transpired. It was three days before Christmas, and I was excited because it was my favorite time of year. But I was even more excited I was being released from the mental institution I had spent three weeks in, and it had been a cold, long month thus far.

I was taken there after a manic, debilitating episode that left me in the care of nurses and psychiatrists who had more control over my decisions than I did. The time I ate; the time I showered; the time I was able to partake in activities; the time I slept. Everything had come down to a clock the institution set – no longer did I live by my own will and time.

I drew pictures on lined paper in the break room locked from the outside during activity time. They were simple pictures drawn with an array of color pencils from a box. Shapes I made up in my head and some I didn't. Like jagged blue stars, backward red moons, and upside-down yellow triangles. All stretched and bent objects that came from a mind, thwarted and misshaped, as I spilled bright colors into the atmosphere to prove that they could not fully restrain my mind - my freedom.

The staff lady watching the room eyed me and told me my drawing was nice. I thanked her, feeling quite proud of myself because I had never drawn before that hospital. I was a writer, dripping black ink onto dull, white paper. Now, I etched brilliant colors outside the black lines. Like the lined canvas before me, my mind had gone outside the lines of reality - enough to put me in a regimented mental hospital where my time was not my own.

My sister opened the passenger door and placed my bag of clothing in the back seat after giving me a long hug. My sister was an artist herself, who only doodled small pictures from time to time between taking care of family and working a job that required no artistic ability.

She dropped me off in front of my mom's quaint home, kissing me on the cheek and saying I love you before I left the car.

"Come see me tomorrow and we'll do something," she said as I took my bag and headed for the front door. I said okay and we parted ways, and I was left to return to a home filled with bad memories of a bipolar episode and the after-effects of a lonely, empty house.

I opened the door to a familiar home - the couch and loveseat still floral, still sitting there. The pictures of all four of us kids on the built-in shelves of the old Victorian home; the small wood table sitting in front of a big kitchen window; the quietness. Nothing had changed, and yet everything had changed.

I went into my dull, colorless room and dropped my bag of clothes on the shabby brown carpet and quickly went into the bathroom to take a shower. Finally, a shower I could shave in, I thought. Finally, the hospital's rules and clock that seemed to forever stand still no longer bound me.

After the shower - after the settling into a home I was so anxious to return to - I realized I had nothing to do. I had no job to go to and no friend to see. Those things had been lost along with my mind for three weeks. But even long before that, as depression had taken a toll on me, and my fervor for those things had dwindled - finally mutating my mind into the undefined shape of bipolar. In turn, I was the girl with a terminated job, friendless, and bound by a mental illness I had no control over.

Left with nothing more to do, I pulled out my sketchbook and new color pencils my sister had purchased for me and began sketching. I let my mind travel to galaxies of stars and moons. I let my imagination be free on blank paper as I floated my pencil across the new canvas like a hang glider. Free.

At that moment in time, there was independence I had not valued before: freedom in my heart that would be short-lived once my mind began to travel outside the lines. This time it would be downward of depression that would last five years long. Radical highs like this would not come again, and I would sink into the low of lows – a place where I would long for colors bursting onto pages to create a world where my mind could float freely into the outer-space of existence.

...

My sister and I drew pictures on the wooden table of her kitchen after the last hospital release when the depression began to sink in, and apathy began to settle like dust on old picture frames. As an older, wiser sister, she realized it was my only outlet during the time of initial numbness; and, being somewhat of an artist herself, she prescribed me the artistic antidote. Later, the numbness would spiral farther than her prescription could draw my heart up from and creating would become but a wishful longing pleasure from my distant past.

We sat there in quiet and - while I drew shapes - she drew a portrait of me with colorful blue hair and purple clothing - the color of royalty.

"That's awesome," I said, truly inspired by the way she spilled vivid paints onto what could be dull, pale white skin and plain brown hair.

But, similar to my images, she had transformed something that could be one-dimensional and drab into something morphed and beautiful - kind of like a mind after it has been broken into pieces then rebuilt with those same pieces only to find that the creation can never exactly be the same.

The rebuilding would take time, but the new creation would be worth all the effort. And eventually, I would pick up the pencil again and freely recreate a shadowed canvas into a beautiful work of art.

Three years earlier…

V
Hands

Hands

I hold my sister's hand like I am holding my own
I sense I have become her reflection
A mirror showing her past
A mirror showing her present
The future of which she does not hold
We hold on to each other like two young girls
In the deep end of a murky pool
She has reached for mine
In a time
When tides of life have risen high
When men have become vast oceans
Uncertainties
Life and death in one
I show her our youth
The giddy girls running through sprinklers
In the summer sun,
Weightless and unbound
I show her our present
The sitting girls,
Shedding skins
Sharing secrets in the dark
Into each other's eyes we look
Like we are searching
For the light
We are one
As beautiful as life
As inevitable as death
Two women of the same kind
Our hands intertwined
Keeping one another afloat

My Sister the Fighter

My sister was always the strong one. Born with a keen sense of insight unlike anyone I have ever known and unafraid to fight anyone who dares to step to her. Her deathly stare pierces like a million knives, and she is quick-witted in times of word-battle. It's those things that are suffocated, buried even, when she relinquishes her strength to another. It's those things I envied.

Unlike me, my sister was always a fighter. On many occasions of my youth, I found myself in a headlock between her arms, surrendering my will to the strength of hers. My measly fist poundings would become slow, soft tapping from weakened arms, and breathing would become heaving as if to plead "mercy." And finally, her army-strength would ease and let go and without a word, we would know who was the strongest of us two.

Also, unlike me, she married a man at a young age – merely 19. He really was a captivating man with a deep, undertaker voice that anyone could distinguish and who could argue his way out of any dispute presented to him. He was intelligent and driven. A strong man, mentally and physically. It was everything she wanted - quite possibly, a match for her undertaking.

So, it was no surprise that cold winter's day when she called. They fought often, in front of me or in front strangers. Being around them was no joy ride. In fact, when I did ride in the back seat of his sports car - with him at the wheel - I watched as my sister turned into a little kid while his angry voice grew like some kind of a mutated animal ready to pounce. My heart rate speeding up like his mustang's engine as my sister shrank right before my eyes.

"I need you to come over right now," she says in a low tone as if she is hiding in a dark closet while strangers take her most sacred belongings.

I quickly drive over to find there are no intruders there, only my sister, who opens the door with her head bowed and my six-month-old nephew on her thin hip. My sister is thin like me, and she has lost even more weight since having her second son.

"What happened?" I ask, feeling the eerie house vibrations creak all around me as if to tell me the secrets of an unsettled home.

"The cops are on the way," she says.

"Why?" I press.

She tells me the secret as if we are two young girls in a dark bedroom again, staring up at a ceiling in the night whispering our inner truths. But alas, we are grown and the secret a shameful one. And the sister who could once beat me in any match of fists and throws for exposing her embarrassing moments to friends has become a young girl, with the heaviness of shame weighing down eyelids and hollow cheeks forbidding smiles.

"You have to leave him," I say, and suddenly I have become the bigger, wiser sister. I feel the thump in my chest like I want to feel the thumping of my fists against a man who has belittled the sister I look up to. My sister just looks down to the floor as a tear escapes and flows down her cheek like a small crooked stream of sadness and truth.

I just wrap my arms around her as my nephew still sits on her hipbones, silently.

"You'll be okay," I say, as strength has begun to mount in my bones and the feeling of having to be strong has settled in my heart.

The cops arrive and I stand there watching like I am the bystander of a car-crash scene.

When they leave, the crooked stream becomes a flood.

"It's embarrassing," my sister says.

"It's okay, let's get out of here." And at that moment in time, I have grown ten times taller than my bigger sister.

We pack her bags and grab her kids and pull out of her driveway like we are secret- escaping refugees after a tragedy of war.

I am at the wheel and my sister in the passenger seat and we ride in silence with the windows cracked. A cool breeze floats through my old Toyota Corolla – a fresh aura of tranquility.

My sister looks up at me.

"Thanks, Eliza," she says with a slight smile then looks back to the road ahead.

And I sense our inherent roles have shifted.

Plum Pie

My sister and I ate bitter plums in the summer sun one afternoon
We sprinkled salt like raindrops on flower fields
To bring out flavor
They stung our teeth like snake bites
On flesh - made to only caress -
But we ate them still
My sister sunk into the dismal of an abysmal marriage
With vows she read out loud "rain or sunshine"
"Hard times, good times"
And all those times in between
When you are sitting alone
Or in a dream
Of some sort
You make-believe plum-purple wounds are bruised-sweetness
Like plum pie in the sky
Let's eat until there is no more
But dreams are like fantasies
When happily ever after becomes another page turned
The heart turns sour
Like those plums in the summer sun
Sting the strength of that thing holding on
When the dark curtain covers the sun
When gravity begins to pull, and fingers begin to dangle
Like hands at alters
Like men and women who falter
When we live in sour-heart homes
How can we ever be free?
Even when kisses become dandelion wishes
Blown away in the wind
And "goodnights" become mouth-watering daydreams
Do not let bitterness rob your reality
Take you from throwing rays of sun
To casting shadows on anyone who comes
Too close
Don't break oaths

With that white-lace girl
We are that stalking shadow we cannot escape
My sister, sit with me in the summer sun
Let's pour sugar on plums
Don't forget the past, but let forgiveness outlast
Because it's freedom after all
After all, isn't that what we all want?
To eat sweet plums, you and me
And sit in the summer sun freely?

The Faith of a Sister

It's summer 2000 and I am on my way to walking the stage of the arena of high school graduation. My sister is in the crowd with the rest of my family and I look up, hearing her shout from the balcony, even amongst the uproar. She has always been able to spot me from the masses, possibly because we look alike. And maybe, right now, she sees herself walking across that stage - the passage of adolescence to womanhood.

I smile then turn to look ahead as luminous lights gleam on the stepping- stone to a brighter future. When they call my name, I hear faint whoops in the background and look toward the very top bungalow where the far-off sound comes from. Later, my sister asks if I heard them. She said she screamed so loud her voice was hoarse. I tell her I barely heard.

...

My sister dropped out of high school at the age of 17, her junior year and my freshman year. She abandoned education to pursue a medical assistant job and soon a man. I was so sad to see her leave, hoping that year we would be able to hang out together on the stone steps in the middle of the high school courtyard. Instead, she soon married the man much older than herself in a courtroom, leaving her goals - perhaps of being some kind of hospital executive - on the high school stepping-stones.

The year she left all of her friends mistook me for her. "I thought you were your sister!" They'd yell, and I would just chuckle under my breath as feelings of solitude sunk my heart.

My sister and I always joked that we were like twins – born of the same mother's womb with the same heart and the same personality. Just like me, she was born with my mother's eyes, although hers are ocean-blue - perhaps to see the lighter side of life. A much more youthful spirit than I, she always had a way of rejuvenating my heart.

Still, people always mistook me for her over the phone with our California accent and lingo of "dude" and "hecka" every other word. And when seeing me walking, they know me by my womanly sway that is just as noticeable as hers.

We also cry at the same movies as, "What Dreams May Come," starring Robin Williams, which became our favorite movie that we watched over again together.

"Oh my God, that's like the saddest movie I've ever seen!" My sister would say.

"Me too!" I'd exclaim. And we'd talk about the part in the movie where the two kids get in a car crash and die suddenly, and suddenly we are transported to that scene and tearing up again.

So, when I crashed at the age of 22, I knew my sister felt it...

...

It's winter of 2004 and I am on a hospital bed with eyes closed and a mouth refusing to open to eat what the nurse is feeding me with a cold spoon. I know it is a nurse because I hear her introduce herself in her foreign African accent; just like I know it is my sister sniffling in the background, although she doesn't talk. I haven't opened my eyes in several days, but I still feel her presence and hear the gasping then all turns dark again.

When I awaken, I am in a hospital room with big sweatpants and an oversized t-shirt on. The man watching our room says I have a visitor. My sister walks in smiling and hugs me tightly.

"Eliza," she says, drawing out the name Eliza like it is a sorrowful note in a sad song.

I sit down on the fluffy couch, hunched over, and she sits across from me poised on a plastic chair like we are separated in some strange fashion. As if I have crossed over to the other side where she is forbidden to come.

She tells me a joke and I laugh because she has that light-hearted way about her. We've always shared the same humor, and at this moment in time, she has lightened the mood - if just for a moment. They call time for visitors to leave and she hugs me tightly again. I watch as she leaves with her head bowed. And I am left alone, sitting on that fluffy couch with an empty plastic chair in front of me.

...

After the hospital, I feel something like a train-wreck has happened in my mind. I watch the movie, "What Dreams May Come," alone in my room, but I can't seem to conjure up tears and feel the feeling I felt when my sister and I watched it. I feel nothing - not even the sun on my face. I can't seem to think for myself, and impulse has replaced decision-making. I cuss more than ever now, and my sister leaves when I do.

She tells me I've "changed," and that I'm "different."

I see anger boil in her the way people who don't understand or fear something begins to burn inside. Then I see the tears roll down her cheeks as she gets up to leave, possibly confused and unable to bear the sights of having lost her sister to a mental crash.

"You're holding yourself back," she tells me. "You can control yourself; you just don't want to."

I tell her she doesn't understand what it is like to be me.

And the aftermath is my twin and me on two separate planets, our heart ripped apart.

...

96

My sister has two small kids now and they come over to see me from time to time. Her sons scream and whine, and it seems she is annoyed all the time. I can't tell if is because of them or me. She tells me she is studying for her GED exam and that it is hard. She's never been good at math and faked it in high school but somehow passed, she says. I sit there thinking about how easy statistics once was for me.

"You're good at math, "she says. And I know she is thinking about the time I taught her algebra to help her pass her math exam. I don't say anything because I feel like my mind is jumbled and I can't put two and two together.

Later she tells me: "You don't know how that affected me," speaking about my mental illness. She begins to tear up again as we sit on my unkempt bed talking under dim, dusty lamplight. It illuminates two unmoving shadows on a blank wall. My room hasn't been cleaned since before the hospital and now smells of thrift store, old clothing.

"When you were in the hospital, a piece of me died."

She looks down as a tear slips from her eyes. She wipes it away quickly. "You don't even know," she concludes, and I sit there in silence, with legs crossed and hands planted on my lap, and a heart, sunken.

…

Depression has a way of separating you from people. I close the door to my room every time my sister leaves the home where I have now become a shut-in. She comes over now and again to see me and takes me shopping – takes me back to those days of her and my shopping, even when I don't feel the thrill of it anymore. But a sense of solace fills me when she does, and it is like life has shifted for that moment in time. We walk side by side as she tries to tell a joke and I laugh a low, fake laugh. But for some reason, the joke helps. And driving in her car with the windows rolled down helps. And the time away from my bedroom – it helps.

It transports me to a different time in my mind as the windows are cracked open, and a draft of breeze floats through her car along with the memories of what it was like to look forward to shopping trips.

She gets mad when I tell her I can't do anything because I am depressed as we sit in the driveway on no particular summer's day.

"You can go back to school," she tells me after I tell her that I want to go back to college for journalism that I started and never finished.

"You can do it, you're just afraid," she presses.

I think she is not in my mind and tell her she doesn't understand like I always do.

"You can do it," she says. "You're just holding yourself back," she tells me again, repeating the same slogan.

I don't tell her I have lost the ability to dream. I don't tell her I can't seem to move from that unkempt bed, and that I can't seem to hear the direction of my own heart.

She tells me again that I am afraid. She has become something of a sub-conscience, always reminding me of my innate fear.

I just sit there and listen and wonder what will come of me and my dreams.

...

At this point, as I sit in my room alone, I think about my many age-old hopes. Then I think about the barrier between getting up and moving, which is this illness. I brush my sister's words away like I am sweeping them under the rug of my matted carpet floor that I haven't vacuumed in years. Clearly, she doesn't see what I see. She sees something like the sister before the crash.

...

"You never listen to me," she says on another shopping trip. "You never listen, and then you do it and you realize I was right."

I just think about how she thinks going back to school is as easy as picking up a pen and paper.

Faith in yourself is like a flame that burns and fuels you. Faith others implant inside you is like that flame ignited. Sometimes it takes someone reaching out to light the match, even when the flame in their own hearts has sizzled down to fumes. My sister has finally passed her GED exam, but she doesn't pursue school after that. She just lets the fire sizzle.

...

"If you graduate, I'll take you to Hawaii," she says on another summer's day, after five years and I have just taken the plunge and enrolled into California State University of Sacramento for the fall semester.

"Really?" I say, excitedly, because I have never been to Hawaii, let alone a vacation.

"Dude, if you graduate, we're going to Hawaii," she says matter-of-factly.

I just chuckle, thinking of how hard it will be to graduate since I'm only enrolled in one art class right now and haven't even begun.

Just the thought of us lying on an island getting tan thrills me; it makes me wish I were in my last semester right now. I look straight ahead through the windshield of my sister's car as the sun sheds light through the glass, creating a dusty stream. A five-year-old dream returned. And suddenly I imagine myself in a cap and gown, smiling with the satisfaction of having come so far.

The vision seems closer than ever now. We seem closer than ever now.

...

Three years later, and we are lying in the sand under a brilliant sun, growing tanner by the minute. Our bronze skin glistens from tanning lotion my sister made sure she put in her duffle bag so we could get "real tan," she says – evidence that we have been to "paradise."

She brought us here on her credit card account and we are staying in the nicest hotel on the beach – the Hyatt.

My sister's head is turned my way. She smiles a lazy smile.

"Dang, you're hecka dark," she says as she looks at me through her dark sunglasses.

"You are too," I say, looking through my matching dark frames and smile back at her. I feel the sun warm my cheek as I lay on my side facing my sister. My heart feels just as warm as that Hawaiian sun.

We joke about our crowded surroundings on Waikiki and she talks about how everyone is laying around like sardines in a can.

"I know!" I say, and we both laugh the same loud laugh from our guts.

We both turn on our backs to face the clear-blue ocean, with our arms crossed behind our heads, as the sunlight shines its rays above us. I hear my sister let out a deep sigh like she is going to sleep. I continue to look in front of me at the waves rolling over again and again and see what looks like a girl swimming in the far distance, headed toward the receding sun.

Three years earlier…

VI

I Have Walked

I have walked

I have walked the stage of florescent lights
A tasseled cap
A black gown
A tear welling up in the eye
Almost falling down
A cheek
Before wiped away
Like the salt of yesterday
I have walked the halls of dark and deranged
A clear tube
A blue gown
Eyes gone dry
For feeling
Somehow left
Somewhere
In the space between
The failing and the falling
I have walked the long haul of recovery
A pill bottle
A glass of water
Five years
Frozen tears
I have walked the stage of second chances
A flipped tassel
A draped cloak
A shed tear for all the years
Of yesterday
Unfelt
A smile for all the stages
I have walked…

Year 2012

The pen in my hand is writing jagged words outside horizontal lines, uncontrollably. Ink spilling scribbles onto a journal I rarely write in because I have the focus span of an ant. I can't seem to stop my erratic writing as I spill fury onto pages that only read of my detest for mental illness all the written words on paper cannot talk me out of. I close the journal as usual then throw it up against a white wall. It drops to the matted floor with its pages now crumpled and flipped open. The ink went dry.

...

My mom and I are sitting at our dull table in the dated kitchen by the big window that sheds light on us. A summer's day like all the rest. Four years have passed since they released me from the last hospital, and I have managed to stay out and free from the cyclical institution. But I sit with my mom often like today and feel something like locked doors surrounding me. I don't feel freedom, rather like a girl stuck on Groundhog Day where the days repeat their same endless orbit. I cannot seem to escape, and my heart still sings something of a mournful tune.

My mom picks up the tea she has set before us and takes a sip from the white mug that matches mine. I do the same and feel its warmth flow like a sweet stream of milk and honey down my throat. I feel the only constant sensation I have felt for four long years that soothes my aching soul like the soft words that come from my mother's lips every time I speak of my mental prison.

"I can't do anything," I tell her. "I can't go back to school. I can't go after my dreams."

"You will when you're ready," she says.

"When! I can't even read or write."

"It will happen."

"When?"

"I'm believing right now. Today."

"No, it's not. It will never happen!"

My mom's bible is in front of her opened to a gold-trimmed page of Job. Some lines are highlighted in yellow and her elegant handwriting has filled up the edges of the pages. A picture of all four of us kids is taped to the left side of the page. I glance down at it for a moment then to the big window that casts light on us through slits of blinds like eyes partially open. I see the pots with my mom's plants inside beginning to sprout.

"God will do it, you'll see."

...

When he calls, his voice rumbles a foreign excitement deep in my gut. We haven't talked in years. I haven't talked to anyone besides my family in years. I'm sitting in my room after time has passed and seasons have cycled for five years and it is summer again. I see the summer sun through the dingy curtain by my bedside and it is 7 p.m. My bed hasn't been made in years, and the room hasn't been dusted in just as long.

He asks how I am, and I say fine.

He asks why I'm not in school and I tell him I can't go back.

"Why not?"

"Because I can't. I can't concentrate, and I'm not healed."

"If you want to do something, you should just do it."

We talk until 8 p.m. and I am beginning to get drowsy. We say goodbye and I am left with the words "want" and "just do it." I glance down to the journal on the floor across from me with torn and blemished pages, and suddenly my heart jumps inside me.

My mom is in the living room when I walk out of my bedroom. Her legs are folded on the couch and a bible unfolded on her lap. She looks up at me with eyes slit and they mirror those window blinds with light shedding through. The house is quiet and still. It has been for years now. But my gut still rumbles something like a fast car ready to jet and speed across a highway on a summer's evening.

"I think I'm going to try to go back to school," I tell her because sometimes it just takes as much as a few short words of belief in somebody to ignite something in your heart.

"You are!"

"Yeah, I think it's time."

"If you think it's time, I believe it's time." And suddenly her belief and my belief coincide like two people in the same dreamscape.

Her smiling eyes reflect light from a dim lamp on one of the side tables, and I turn to go fill out a school application.

...

They've built onto California State University of Sacramento since I last attended. A new grey building stands tall as kids walk in and out of its sliding doors. Trees shade kids sitting on benches underneath as I pass by on the twisting turning paths.

I'm twenty-eight and feel nerves mixed with excitement like on my first day of junior high school. I wear ripped jeans and a t-shirt like the kids sitting on the benches chatting with one another. Other than that, the campus is quiet, and the birds chirp back and forth overhead.

Summer school has let out and won't start again until fall. I travel along the path as I pass one familiar sign. It reads "Communications" and I am reminded of the classrooms inside where I once sat attentively in the front row, writing straight words across the clean-lined paper - notes about journalist ethics and editing. My nerves begin to pick up their pace, as my feet follow, and now I have traveled along this path in a circle and I am back where I started by the grey building.

I wonder how I will ever do this school thing again. I can't even find my way. The sun is burning my forehead now and the sweat under my arms is dampening my t-shirt. But I follow the path again.

I pass by another sign that reads "Lassen Hall," and my mind travels back to the time I brought my transcripts here as a 20-year-old ready to transfer to this state university with butterflies in my stomach and dreams of conquering the world.

I follow the signs that lead to Lassen Hall.

It has familiar art along its walls, and it reads on a small printed sign, "Admissions."

I walk through the double doors as it opens wide for me. Inside is cool and quiet as kids line up in the office of admissions. I follow the signs to the desk of transferring students as my nerves have now sped up with my heartbeat and I am that junior high school student again.

The receptionist greets me.

I am nearly shaking as I walk up to the front desk like a kid in front of a classroom of gawking peers.

"How can I help you?" She asks.

"Hi, I'm returning student. And I'd like to see how to reapply."

She directs me to a computer, unlike the archaic paper applications of years ago. Another student is in front of the identical screen beside it. I walk up to the screen as my heartbeat still pounds in my chest like resounding drums, and I feel closer than ever to my next step in life – a step in the direction of normality. I glance to the right where the young girl by my side is filling out the online application in frayed ripped jeans and a t-shirt.

Two years later…

VII
Birthing Light

Birthing light

The girl with the closed mouth
Has worlds to say
She has something like the midnight sky
In her throat
Sprinkled stars glisten
Guide the way to the moon of her heart
She has lived the darkness
A world where demons shut her voice in
Lock door of her essence
Their presence
Pulls her down like gravity
Trap her to an earth they say was never hers
A realm where freedom to speak
Seems foreign language
Where you cannot speak up
Speak self
Shout moon
And stars
Of self-proclamation
But she
Is capable of birthing light
Into existence
Merely by
Opening her mouth
To speak

Year 2015

Two years have passed now since college graduation. I'm sitting in my mom's kitchen on a summer's morning as the white sun sheds light through the open window next to my mom and me. It's been four years since I broke out of my depression and 12 years since I was released from the last mental institution. I look at my mom from across the small glass table in the kitchen that reflects a summer's sunlight. A new gas stove and fridge sit next to walls that have never witnessed the screams of a mentally ill girl.

We've moved from the old Victorian house into a new home in a much quieter neighborhood on the other side of town. I look out the window where streams of light glisten on a clear pool the color of pastel blue. My mom's pots of plants sit in front of it, and flowers spread their petals wide as if spreading fingers waiting on food to be placed. My mom will go out to water them soon, but for now, we sit and talk about life and past.

"You've come so far," my mom says with her hand resting on an open bible she has had ever since my mental illness, now torn and cracked.

"I know," I say.

"But God helped you out of that."

I think back about sitting in a room on a messy bed under a dim lamplight waiting on the ship of mental illness to sail. I think about my mom and I sitting together in the kitchen of our old Victorian home talking about healing as the sun sheds light on my mom's bright eyes that seem to be a mirror reflecting my visceral doubt and depression back at me.

My mom's face has more wrinkles and crow's feet gather next to her smiling eyes, but we still look alike. Her curly black hair has turned salt and pepper now, but it is still long – longer than my curly brown hair. Clearly, she has found the fountain of youth, which seems to be a trait of her God-like attributes.

"I know," I say. "I just don't know what to do next."

My laptop is open in front of me to a poem I am writing that seems to be pulling me towards it like a crying child. I've written poetry since I was a seven-year-old girl. But the dark days of depression put a halt to that, and for five years I could not bring myself to write a single good word. Now I often write short prose and poetry and eloquent words have returned to me like a bird to its nest.

"Read me your poem," my mom says.

I read her a poem I've titled, "The War," that describes a girl's war with her mind. I feel a warm tear trickle down my cheek.

"Excellent," she says when the last word strings from my lips and the room falls silent like an audience waiting for an opera singer.

"I've always said your writing is like a symphony," she says. "I can just hear it when you read."

"Thanks, mom," I say as a smile softens my cheekbones and the tear dries up. "I just don't know what I'll do next."

"You'll find something."

I look up to the mantel in the dining area on top of the fireplace and see my diploma. It sits next to a poem I wrote and framed for my mom for Mother's Day, which now seems so long ago. I feel a sinking in my chest as I see the dust beginning to settle on the green cover of my diploma. I think back about all my 20-year-old dreams of conquering the world. I don't let my mom see me wrestling to keep tears in, nor that thing stuck in my throat. I just look down at the small print on the screen in front of me and read back over, "The War."

…

Everything has changed since I was twenty. No one goes to the I-street library downtown anymore to check out books. The world has shifted to iPhones and online, and journalism seems to be a lost art.

I'm scrolling the web looking at fashion blogs and thinking about my dreams of being a fashion journalist. Fashion has changed like it always does, and we are back to crop tops and bell-bottom jeans like the days before the years I lost my mind.

My chin is resting on my hand as I stare at words and pictures on the screen thinking about how the day will go. I have no plans and purpose seems like a word from far away worlds I once dreamed of while I was away in prison of my mind.

Purpose. The screen in front of me is looking back at me as my eyes shift to the word, "Blog," at the top of a pretty girl with brown hair and a sundress on.

Suddenly, the word and the world make sense. I feel an awakening in myself as if I had been sleeping all along.

If journalism has shifted to online, then online is where I should be.

I close the blog window and open a blank page of word documents and begin moving my fingers as quickly as the thoughts flash through my mind like a motion picture.

...

"I'm going to start a blog!" I tell my mom when she comes home from work.

"You are! What kind?"

"A poetry blog. I've always written poetry, so I just thought I'd start a blog. That's where everything is going anyway."

My mom smiles her gifted smile.

"I know you can do it, Mija. I'm so happy for you."

I retreat to the kitchen and sit down at the glass table and my mom joins me with a cup of steaming tea.

"If I'm going to start a blog, then I have to go to a poetry venue. And if I go to a venue then I have to get up there. I have to at least once to write about it – about the feeling."

The memory of my 19-year-old self is in my mind now and I am standing in front of a class of peers trying to recite a presentation. My voice is cracking, and my hands are shaking like one of those rattling dolls, and I am terrified. The class is looking at me, and I just know they are laughing in their minds. I speak low and muffled, and I realize I can't do this public speaking thing again.

"I don't know. I don't want to get up there," I resolve.

I'm a shy person in general. All my years in school I was nervous. My face flushed red every time the teacher called on me. Even at the university, I was like the girl wanting to run and hide every time I felt my words come out stupidly - like a stumbling fool. It's like I can never articulate what I am thinking, and I have become that junior high school student again.

"You can do it. I believe in you," my mom says.

"I guess it doesn't hurt to do it this once," I resolve, although my heart is now beating through my chest and not even my mom's soothing voice of solace can calm it.

I think about a large crowd of gawking eyes and booing. I think about words that will cease to come out because I have become a statue and the words frozen in midair. I stare off in a daydream, looking out the open window at the wind ruffling the rose bush's leaves, and my heart is anxious and excited at the same time.

...

Poet's Café is like a mecca for poets. That's what I realize when I open the jingling door and go to sit down at a round table by a blue wall with paintings hung on it.

I am wearing my favorite colorful scarf wrapped around my head as a tribute to my young adult days of hip-hop beats and urban style - the days before mental illness, when youth was vigorous, cultured and free.

I look like I fit right into this poetic scene, although my hands are shaking uncontrollably, and my stomach has become a knot being tightened every time I look around. There are several tables in the room occupied by strangers who have glanced my way. One man is holding a piece of paper and I see his lips moving and hear him mumble words under his breath. I look down at my paper with a poem I wrote but can't seem to make out the words because my hands won't stop shaking. And I have become a rattling doll with sweaty hands.

A waitress in an apron and braids in her hair comes up to me.

116

"Can I get you anything dear?"

I say yes and order a smoothie. She smiles a charming smile and goes back behind the wooden bar that looks like it is from one of those western films.

I look down at my paper, trying to take in breaths as the knot pulls tighter. Just this once, I tell myself.

A lady in fishnet stockings and a red dress comes up to me.

"Would you like to sign up for the open mic?"

"Yeah."

She hands me a clipboard with drawn lines numbered. My eyes jot up and down the paper. Slots are open on the first few lines, but I sign up on the fifth one as I breathe heavily, and the shaking has become unrestrained.

"Is this your first time?"

"Yeah," I say, looking up to her avoiding eye contact for too long. I don't like eye contact. I don't like it when people gaze into my eyes like they are looking to find some kind of dark secret behind them.

The room is beginning to get more and more full. I try to slurp down my smoothie but can't seem to enjoy its flavor or hold it without it nearly spilling because my hands can't seem to take hold of themselves. Just this once, I think.

"Welcome to Poet's Café!" The lady in fishnet stockings and a tight red dress yells from behind a microphone. She is standing on the stage in front of the room with a pink drink in her hand as the crowd roars.

"We're going to get the open mic started."

My heart rate has sped up to miles beyond my thoughts. I look down at my paper making a shuffling sound that I can't seem to quiet like my thoughts.

Several poets have gotten up and spent their five minutes of fame they were allotted by the host. Each one is unique and speaks eloquently. More eloquent than me, I think.

Four poets have gone up. I feel like my heart is going to jump out of my chest. I swallow but my throat has gone dry.

"Give it up for Eliza!" The host yells and the crowd claps off-key.

I go up to the stage as I see from my peripheral, eyes following me like they are waiting to see me trip and fall.

"Can you guys hear me?" I ask as I feel my voice has shrunk down to the size of a mouse.

"Yeah," a guy in the front row says.

"This is my first time here," I say, and the crowd begins to yell and clap higher than my first introduction. Somehow, that makes the nerves ease and my face bones relax. And I open my mouth.

I read the poem I have written just for the occasion titled, "Under the Trees." It's a poem about the area I grew up in, in the "City of Trees," where we once lived in an old Victorian house - the same house I once experienced the horrors of mental illness. I don't tell them the gory story behind the poem. I don't tell them the drug addiction I once witnessed on that block or that I lost my mind under those trees. I just keep the story stored in my heart and continue letting the playful words trickle from my lips.

My hands are shaking again, and I notice the paper won't stop moving and I just know they are looking at nerves manifest on my flushed face.

I don't look at the crowd. I just keep my eyes stuck to the paper.

When I am done, I say thank you and hear the crowd whistle and clap loudly again. A rush like a gust of wind blows through my system. I feel my nerves begin to settle down and I walk back to my table.

"Good job," a man in a fedora says.

I smile slightly but feel the glee of the gifted child my mom spoke of.

The host goes back up the stage and raises her pink drink in the air.

"If you guys want to see Eliza come back, clap your hands!"

The crowd roars.

I continue to smile, and nerves are replaced by thrill as if I have just gotten off a roller coaster. I look down at my paper to the poem I have titled, "Under the Trees." And the wind still blows within me.

…

My mom is sleeping on the green couch when I walk through the door of our suburban home. Moving here was like a breath of fresh air I hadn't breathed in years. I left much of my darkness under the trees of our old neighborhood when I moved with my mom to this middle-class neighborhood where small trees have sprouted but not grown into their fruition. Kind of like dreams that begin to grow then, if watered enough, turn into manifestations.

I see my mom's eyelids open slightly.

"Guess what mom?"

She immediately sits up.

"What sweetheart?"

"I got up there! It went good!"

"Oh, I'm so happy sweetheart."

"I know. I'm going to do it again."

My mom smiles her sleepy smile.

"I'm so happy," she says, then lays back down with her head facing the ceiling and closes her eyes while her mouth is still moving like she is talking to God of the night sky.

I go into my room with walls a shade or two lighter than the dusted over room I once experienced the depression-nightmare in. I pull out my laptop and begin letting my fingers dance on the keyboard to my heart song written in poetic verses. I think about my childhood journal of poetry written to God and feel the same peace I felt like a mother holding her child to her bosom. I think about years of inhibited writing feats and the journey to healing and feel my tears-turned-words pour over the pages as if something has just opened up within. And my heart just keeps singing.

...

The year has been a roller coaster, rising high with the crowd's cheers at Poet's Café then falling with butterflies in my stomach. The lows are downtimes of writing poetry and reciting it in my room – which is not lows at all. These days, I feel purpose mixed with excitement like cake batter ready to throw into the oven. I wonder what will be made of it. I wonder if there is a sweet sensation at the end and what it will look like when it is here.

I always wanted to do something special. But my days of darkness suffocated much of my dreams and I doubted I would ever be able to do anything I wanted to when I was that 20-year-old girl. I have seen my mother's passage through time: how she has overcome many of her demons, been a survivor and chosen to follow God. I've seen my sister's – how she too has been a survivor and chosen her family.

I've dug tunnels in search of myself; looked within men and soul-searched within religion. I too am a survivor and overcomer, but me - I have chosen to follow my heart.

Now here I am after time has passed and the days of church and mental illness too, and I am that hopeful girl again.

Fred, one of the hosts at Poet's Café has asked me to be a featured artist. My stomach is once again in knots, but this time it squeezes the fruit-juice of excitement. My computer is open to the document of words I have pieced together seamlessly because it is like words just fall from the sky and into my mind when I am in front of a screen. My mom says I'm a natural; that I have a gift. She still smiles when I read her my poetry as we sit by the kitchen window in the soft summer's sunlight.

...

Poet's café is packed when we arrive. I've brought my mom here for the first time so she can see me on stage.

Nerves fill my stomach like un-still waters ready to break through a tunnel. Poets fill the room – some say they have come out just to see me and devote some of their poetry to me. I smile widely like a child opening a Christmas gift.

"When I found out I was the first person to have Eliza as a featured poet, I was honored," Fred says in his high pitch tone.

"Everyone – Eliza!" He yells.

I get up and feel thrill rush through me like the height of that roller coaster and I have reached the top of its summit.

I walk up on stage as the audience cheers loudly in the background.

I go to open my mouth and look into the crowd that has gone silent like an auditorium waiting for a symphony to begin playing the song of angels. And my heart begins singing the song it has waited to all along.

Freedom

Freedom exists
In the way I move through the wind
The way

My hips sway like seesaw
And air
Blows this hair
Like a flag in the wind
I am the girl once tied to the chair
With ropes soaked in poison of annihilation
Light of a match
Blew fire out
In my eye
And I
Have seen the dark
Enough to know light
That rises like irises
To the sun
Freedom exists
In my heart-shaped lips
Opening
To exhale words of wisdom
Once locked away
In a dusty journal without a key
Freedom exists
In the way my feet move
To the beat of that thing
In my chest
Freedom exists
In arms raised high and wide to the sky
Like the eye
Of a wide-eyed child
Freedom exists
In the children in me
Freedom exists
In the dreams of these

Author Bio

A native of Sacramento, California, Izzy Lala is a poet, writer and artist striving to encourage and inspire people to follow their hearts. She earned a bachelor's degree from California State University, Sacramento, where she studied journalism and studio art. A firm believer in "following your heart," Izzy Lala shifted gears after college to pursue her first passion of poetry as a spoken word artist. Her topics include family, mental health and relationships, of which she can be found performing on stage at any given poetry venue in Sacramento. She currently writes poetry and fiction stories, sprinkling in personal style and unique perspective. Her debut book, *Her Heart Song*, is a collection of poetry and excerpted fiction stories that evolved organically out of her desire to write a relatable story that lends itself to hope. Her desire is that her voice will offer a sense of hope and encourage people to find their own way hope and healing.

More information about her and her blog can be found at izzylala.com

Made in the USA
Columbia, SC
25 February 2020